Daisy Miller

A COMEDY IN THREE ACTS

HENRY JAMES

DAISY MILLER

A Comedy

IN THREE ACTS

BOSTON AND NEW YORK
HOUGHTON, MIFFLIN AND COMPANY
The Riverside Press, Cambridge
1899

The Riverside Press, Cambridge, Mass., U. S. A.
Printed by H. O. Houghton & Company.

Dramatis Personæ.

———◆———

FREDERICK WINTERBOURNE.

CHARLES REVERDY.

GIACOMO GIOVANELLI.

EUGENIO.

RANDOLPH MILLER.

MRS. COSTELLO.

MADAME DE KATKOFF.

ALICE DURANT.

MRS. WALKER.

DAISY MILLER.

A WAITER.

8931

DAISY MILLER

𝔄 𝔊𝔬𝔪𝔢𝔡𝔶

ACT FIRST.

Garden and terrace of an hotel on the Lake of Geneva. The portico of the hotel to the left, with steps leading up to it. In the background a low parapet dividing the garden from the lake, and divided itself by a small gate opening upon a flight of steps which are supposed to descend to a pier. Beyond this a distant view of mountains and of the lake, with the Château de Chillon. Orange-trees in green tubs, benches, a few small tables and chairs.

SCENE FIRST.

MADAME DE KATKOFF, EUGENIO.

MADAME DE KATKOFF, coming in as if a little startled, with a French book in a pink cover under her arm.

I believe he means to speak to me! He is capable of any impertinence.

EUGENIO, following slowly, handsomely dressed, with a large watchguard, and a courier's satchel over his shoulder. He takes off his hat and bows obsequiously, but with a certain mock respect.

Madame does me the honor to recognize me, I think.

MADAME DE KATKOFF.

Certainly I recognize you. I never forget my servants, especially (with a little laugh) the faithful ones !

EUGENIO.

Madame's memory is perhaps slightly at fault in leading her to speak of me as a servant !

MADAME DE KATKOFF.

What were you, then ? A friend, possibly ?

EUGENIO.

May I not say that I was, at least on a certain occasion, an adviser ?

MADAME DE KATKOFF.

In the way of occasions, I remember only the one on which I turned you out of the house.

EUGENIO.

You remember it with a little regret, I hope.

MADAME DE KATKOFF.

An immense deal — that I had n't dismissed you six months sooner !

EUGENIO.

I comprehend the regret of Madame. It was in those six months that an incident occurred — (He pauses.)

MADAME DE KATKOFF.

An incident ?

EUGENIO.

An incident which it is natural that Madame should not have desired to come to the knowledge of persons occupying a position, however humble, near Madame.

MADAME DE KATKOFF, aside.

He is more than impertinent — he is dangerous. (Aloud.) You are very audacious. You took away a great deal of money.

EUGENIO.

Madame appears still to have an abundance.

MADAME DE KATKOFF, looking at him a moment.

Yes, I have enough.

EUGENIO, smiling.

Madame is to be congratulated! I have never ceased to take an interest in Madame. I have followed her — at a distance.

MADAME DE KATKOFF.

The greater the distance, the better!

EUGENIO, significantly.

Yes, I remember that Madame was very fond of her privacy. But I intrude as little as possible. I have duties at present which give me plenty of occupation. Not so much, indeed, as when I was in the employment of Monsieur de Katkoff: that was the busiest part of my life. The Russians are very exacting — the Americans are very easy!

MADAME DE KATKOFF.

You are with Americans now?

EUGENIO.

Madame sees that she *is* willing to talk! I am travelling with a family from New York — a family of three persons.

MADAME DE KATKOFF.

You have no excuse, then, for detaining me; you know where to find conversation.

EUGENIO.

Their conversation is not so agreeable as that of Madame! (With a slight change of tone.) I know more about you than you perhaps suspect.

MADAME DE KATKOFF.

I know what you know.

EUGENIO.

Oh, I don't allude to Madame's secrets. I should never be so indiscreet! It is not a secret to-day that Madame has a charming villa on this lovely lake, about three miles from Geneva.

MADAME DE KATKOFF.

No, that is not a secret.

EUGENIO.

And that though she leads a life of elegant seclusion, suited to the mourning which she has never laid aside — though she has lightened it a little — since she became a widow, Madame does not entirely shut her doors. She receives a few privileged persons.

MADAME DE KATKOFF, aside.

What on earth is he coming to? (Aloud.) Do you aspire to be one of them?

EUGENIO.

I should count upon it the day I should have something particular to say to Madame. But that day may never come.

MADAME DE KATKOFF.

Let us hope so!

EUGENIO.

Let us hope so! Meanwhile Madame is in a position to know as well as myself that — as I said just now — the Americans are very easy.

MADAME DE KATKOFF.

The Americans?

EUGENIO.

Perhaps, after all, Madame does n't find them so? Her most privileged visitor is of that nationality! Has he discovered — like me — that the Russians are very exacting?

MADAME DE KATKOFF, looking at him a moment, then quickly, though with an effort.

The Russians, when their antagonists go too far, can be as dangerous as any one else! I forget *your* nationality.

EUGENIO.

I am not sure that Madame ever knew it. I'm an Italian Swiss, a native of the beautiful city of Lugano. Is Madame acquainted with Lugano? If she should go that way, I recommend the Hôtel Washington: always our Americans, you see! The Russians? They are the most dangerous people I know, and we gentlemen who take charge of families know everything.

MADAME DE KATKOFF.

You had better add frankly that you traffic in your knowledge.

EUGENIO.

What could be more just? It costs us a good deal to get it.

MADAME DE KATKOFF, to herself, after a pause.

It is best to know the worst, and have done with it. (Aloud.) How much do you want?

EUGENIO.

How much do I want for what? For keeping quiet about Mr. Winterbourne, so that his family shan't think he's wasting his time, and come out from America to bring him home? You see I know even his name! He's supposed to be at Geneva for purposes of study.

MADAME DE KATKOFF.

How much do you want to go away and never let me see you again? Be merciful. Remember that I'm not rich.

EUGENIO.

I know exactly the fortune of Madame! She is not rich,

for very good reasons — she was exceedingly extravagant in her youth! On the other hand, she is by no means in misery. She is not rich, like the American lady — the amiable Mrs. Miller — whom I have at present the honor to serve; but she is able to indulge herself with the usual luxuries.

MADAME DE KATKOFF.

It would be a luxury to get rid of you!

EUGENIO.

Ah, I 'm not sure that Madame can afford that; that would come under the head of extras! Moreover, I 'm not in want of money. The amiable Mrs. Miller —

MADAME DE KATKOFF, interrupting.

The amiable Mrs. Miller is as great a fool as I?

EUGENIO.

I should never think of comparing her with Madame! Madame has much more the appearance of one who is born to command. It is for this reason that I approached her with the utmost deliberation. I recognized her three days ago, the evening she arrived at the hotel, and I pointed her out to Mrs. Miller as a Russian lady of great distinction, whose husband I had formerly the honor to serve in a very confidential position. Mrs. Miller has a daughter even more amiable than herself, and this young lady was profoundly impressed with the distinguished appearance of Madame.

MADAME DE KATKOFF.

Her good opinion is doubtless of great value; but I suppose it 's hardly to assure me of that —

EUGENIO.

I may add that I did n't permit myself to make any further remarks.

MADAME DE KATKOFF.

And your discretion's an example of what you are capable of doing? I should be happy to believe it, and if you have not come to claim your reward —

EUGENIO.

My reward? My reward shall be this : that we leave the account open between us! (Changing his tone entirely.) Let me speak to you very frankly. Some eight years ago, when you were thirty years old, you were living at Dresden.

MADAME DE KATKOFF.

I was living at Dresden, but I was not thirty years old.

EUGENIO.

The age does n't matter — we will call it twenty, if you like ; that makes me younger, too. At that time I was under your roof ; I was the confidential servant, on a very exceptional footing, of M. de Katkoff. He had a great deal of business — a great deal of diplomatic business ; and as he employed me very often to write for him — do you remember my beautiful hand? — I was not so much a servant as a secretary. At any rate, I was in a position to observe that you had a quarrel with your husband.

MADAME DE KATKOFF.

In a position? I should think you were! He paid you to spy upon me.

EUGENIO.

To spy upon you?

MADAME DE KATKOFF.

To watch me — to follow me — to calumniate me.

EUGENIO, smiling.

That's just the way you used to talk! You were always violent, and that gave one an advantage.

MADAME DE KATKOFF.

All this is insupportable. Please to spare me your reminiscences, and come to the point.

EUGENIO.

The point is this — that I got the advantage of you then, and that I have never lost it ! Though you did n't care for your husband, you cared for some one else ; and M. de Katkoff — with my assistance, if you will — discovered the object of your preference. Need I remind you of what followed, the day this discovery became known to you ? Your surprise was great, because you thought yourself safe ; but your anger was even greater. You found me for a moment in your path, and you imagined — for that moment — that I was a Russian serf. The mistake had serious consequences. You called me by the vilest of names — and I have never forgotten it !

MADAME DE KATKOFF.

I thank you for reminding me of my contempt. It was extremely sweet.

EUGENIO.

It made you very reckless. I got possession of two letters, addressed to the person I speak of, and singularly rash compositions. They bear your signature in full.

MADAME DE KATKOFF.

Can there be any better proof that I have nothing to be ashamed of ?

EUGENIO.

You were not ashamed then, because, as I have already remarked, you were reckless. But to-day you are wise.

MADAME DE KATKOFF, proudly.

Whatever I have said — I have always signed !

EUGENIO.

It 's a habit I appreciate.   One of those letters I gave to
M. de Katkoff; the other — the best — I kept for myself.

MADAME DE KATKOFF.

What do you mean by the best?

EUGENIO.

I mean — the worst!

MADAME DE KATKOFF.

It can't be very bad.

EUGENIO, smiling.

Should you like me to submit it to a few of your friends?

MADAME DE KATKOFF, aside.

Horrible man!   (Aloud.)   That 's the point, then : you
wish to sell it.

EUGENIO.

No ; I only wish you to know I have it.

MADAME DE KATKOFF.

I knew that already.   What good does it do you ?

EUGENIO.

You suspected it, but you did n't know it.   The good it
does me is this — that when, as sometimes happens to us
poor members of a despised and laborious class, I take stock
of my prospects and reckon up the little advantages I may
happen to possess, I like to feel that particular one among
them.

MADAME DE KATKOFF.

I see — you regard it as a part of your capital.   But you
draw no income.

EUGENIO.

Ah, the income, Madame, is accumulating !

MADAME DE KATKOFF.

If you are trying to frighten me, you don't — very much !

EUGENIO.

Very much — no! But enough is as good as a feast. There is no telling what may happen. We couriers have our ups and downs, and some day I may be in distress. Then, and only then, if I feel a pinch, I shall call on Madame. For the present —

MADAME DE KATKOFF.

For the present, you only wish to insult me!

EUGENIO.

Madame does injustice to my manners : they are usually much appreciated. For the rest of the time that we remain under the same roof — so to speak — I shall not again disturb your meditations.

MADAME DE KATKOFF.

Be so good as to leave me.

EUGENIO.

I wish Madame a very good morning! (He goes into the hotel.)

MADAME DE KATKOFF, stands a moment, thinking.

That's what it is to have been a fool — for a single moment! That moment reëchoes through eternity. He has shaken my nerves, and in this wretched garden one is always observed. (Exit into the hotel.)

SCENE SECOND.

MRS. COSTELLO, MISS DURANT, CHARLES REVERDY.

They come out of the hotel as Madame de Katkoff passes into it, looking at her attentively.

REVERDY, who carries a camp-stool.

That's the biggest swell in the house — a Russian princess!

MRS. COSTELLO.

A Russian princess is nothing very great. We have found one at every hotel.

REVERDY.

Well, this is the best of them all. You would notice her anywhere.

MRS. COSTELLO.

The best bred people are the people you notice least.

REVERDY.

She 's very quiet, any way. She speaks to no one.

MRS. COSTELLO.

You mean by that that no one speaks to her.

REVERDY, aside.

The old lady 's snappish this morning : hanged if I 'll stand it ! (Aloud.) No one speaks to her, because no one ventures to.

MISS DURANT.

You ventured to, I think, and she did n't answer you. That 's what you mean by her being quiet !

REVERDY.

She dropped her fan, and I picked it up and gave it to her. She thanked me with a smile that was a poem in itself : she did n't need to speak !

MRS. COSTELLO.

You need n't mind waiting on Russian princesses. Your business is to attend to us — till my nephew comes.

REVERDY, looking at his watch.

As I understand you, he 's already due.

MRS. COSTELLO.

He 's a quarter of an hour late. We are waiting breakfast.

MISS DURANT.

I'm afraid the delay will bring on one of your headaches.

MRS. COSTELLO.

I have one already, so it does n't matter!

REVERDY, aside.

Very convenient, those headaches! (Aloud.) Won't you sit down, at least? (Offering camp-stool.) You know I don't come out for three minutes without our little implement.

MRS. COSTELLO.

I don't care for that; I'll sit on a bench.

REVERDY, aside.

She insists on my bringing it, and yet she won't use it! (The ladies seat themselves, and he places himself between them, astride the camp-stool. He continues, aloud.) If Mr. Winterbourne is already due, my holiday has legally begun.

MISS DURANT.

You won't lose anything by waiting. After he comes you will be at perfect liberty.

REVERDY.

Oh, yes, after that you won't look at me, I suppose! Miss Durant is counting very much on Mr. Winterbourne.

MRS. COSTELLO.

And I am counting very much on Miss Durant. You are to be very nice to him, you know.

MISS DURANT.

That will depend on how I like him.

MRS. COSTELLO.

That's not what I brought you to Europe for — to make conditions. Besides, Frederick's a perfect gentleman.

MISS DURANT.

You seem to wish me to promise to marry him. I must wait till he asks me, you know.

REVERDY.

He will ask you if Mrs. Costello bids him.   He is evidently in excellent training.

MRS. COSTELLO.

I have n't seen him for ten years: at that time he was a model nephew.

REVERDY.

I should n't wonder if he were to turn out a regular "hard" one.   That would be a jolly lark!

MRS. COSTELLO.

That 's not his reputation.   Moreover, he has been brought up in Geneva, the most moral city in Europe.

REVERDY.

You can 't tell anything from that.   Here am I, brought up in New York — and we all know what New York is. Yet where can you find a more immaculate young man ?   I have n't a fault — I 'm ashamed of myself !

MISS DURANT.

If Mr. Winterbourne is a little wild, I shan't like him any the less.   Some faults are very charming.

REVERDY.

Tell me what they are, and I 'll try and acquire them.

MRS. COSTELLO.

My dear Alice, I 'm startled by your sentiments.   I have tried to form your taste . . .

MISS DURANT.

Yes, but you have only cultivated my dislikes.   Those are a few of my preferences.

REVERDY.

Tell us a few more of them — they sound awfully spicy !

MISS DURANT.

I 'm very fond of a certain indifference. I like men who are not always running after you with a camp-stool, and who don't seem to care whether you like them or not.

MRS. COSTELLO.

If you like rude men, they are very easily found. If I did n't know you were a very nice girl, I should take you for — I don't know what!

REVERDY.

Miss Durant's remarks are addressed to me, and between you two ladies it 's hard to know what to do. You want me to be always at your elbow, and you make a great point of the camp-stool. Will you have it a little, for a change? (Getting up and offering it. Mrs. Costello refuses with a gesture.) I don't offer it to Miss Alice; we have heard what *she* thinks of it!

MISS DURANT.

I did n't speak of that piece of furniture: I spoke of the person who carries it.

REVERDY.

The person who carries the camp-stool? Is that what I 've come to be known by? Look here, my dear friends, you ought to engage a courier.

MRS. COSTELLO.

To cheat us out of our eyes? Thank you very much!

REVERDY.

A courier with a gorgeous satchel, and a feather in his hat — like those ladies from Schenectady!

MRS. COSTELLO.

So that he might smoke in our faces, as he does in theirs, and have his coffee with us after dinner, as he does with them? They have ruined a good servant.

MISS DURANT.

They treat him as an equal; they make him their companion.

REVERDY.

But they give him handsome wages — which is more than you do me!

MISS DURANT.

I have no doubt they give him little tokens of affection, and locks of their hair. But that makes them only the more dreadful!

MRS. COSTELLO.

I 'm glad to see, my dear, that your taste is coming back to you!

REVERDY.

Oh, if taste consists in demolishing Miss Daisy Miller, she can take the prize.

MISS DURANT.

Demolishing her? I should be sorry to take that trouble. I think her very vulgar: that 's all!

MRS. COSTELLO.

Miss Daisy Miller? Is that her distinguished name?

REVERDY, aside.

Ah, we can't all be named Costello!

MRS. COSTELLO.

They are the sort of Americans that one does one's duty by not accepting.

REVERDY.

Ah, you don't accept her?

MRS. COSTELLO.

I would if I could — but I can't. One should let Europeans know —

REVERDY.

One should let them know?

MRS. COSTELLO.

That we are not all like that.

REVERDY.

They can see it for themselves : she's charmingly pretty.

MISS DURANT.

You are extremely impertinent.

REVERDY, aside.

I put in one that time. (Aloud.) I can't help it; she's lovely.

MRS. COSTELLO.

And is the mamma lovely, too? Has any one ever seen the mamma?

REVERDY.

She's sick in bed — she's always sick.

MISS DURANT.

The courier sits with her, and gives her her medicine.

REVERDY.

I hope you call that devoted, then?

MRS. COSTELLO.

It does n't matter, because the head of the family is the little boy. He orders the dinner; he has the best seat in the carriage.

REVERDY.

He's the most amusing little specimen. He has the heart of a patriot in the body of a — (Hesitates for a word.)

MISS DURANT.

In the body of a grasshopper!

REVERDY.

He hops a good deal, or, rather, I should say, he flies; for there is a good deal of the spread-eagle about him.

MISS DURANT.

He leaves his toys all over the hotel; I suppose you would say his plumes.

REVERDY.

Well, he's a dauntless American infant; a child of nature and of freedom.

MRS. COSTELLO.

Oh, nature and freedom! We have heard too much of *them*.

REVERDY.

Wait till you are stopped at the New York custom-house! The youthful Miller and I have struck up a friendship: he introduced me to his sister.

MRS. COSTELLO.

You don't mean to say you spoke to her!

REVERDY.

Spoke to her? Yes, indeed — and she answered me.

MISS DURANT.

She was not like the Russian princess!

REVERDY.

No, she's as little as possible like the Russian princess; but she's very charming in another style. As soon as Mr. Winterbourne arrives (and you must excuse me for saying that he takes a deuce of a time about it), I shall console myself for the loss of your society by plunging into that of the Millers.

MRS. COSTELLO.

You won't lose us, Mr. Reverdy: you can console yourself with me.

REVERDY.

Oh, thank you!

MRS. COSTELLO.

Frederick will devote himself to Alice.

MISS DURANT.

We had better wait till he comes! I have no patience with his delay.

MRS. COSTELLO.

Neither have I, my dear; but I may as well take the opportunity of remarking that a young lady should n't seem too eager . . .

MISS DURANT.

Too eager?

MRS. COSTELLO.

For the arrival of a gentleman.

MISS DURANT.

I see what you mean — more reserve. But simply before you . . .

REVERDY.

And before me, please. Am I nobody?

MISS DURANT.

Nobody at all!

REVERDY.

Well, I don't care, for I descry in the distance the adorable Miss Miller!

MISS DURANT.

I 'm glad she 's in the distance.

REVERDY.

Ah, but she 's coming this way.

MISS DURANT, quickly.

I forbid you to speak to her.

REVERDY, aside.

Ah, then I *am* somebody? (Aloud.) I can't cut the poor girl, you know.

MISS DURANT.

You need n't see her.   You can look at me.

MRS. COSTELLO.

She 's always wandering about the garden — the image of idleness and inanity.

REVERDY.

She 's not as serious as we, nor as well occupied, certainly ; but she 's bored to death.   She has got no one to flirt with.

MISS DURANT.

She shall not flirt with you, at any rate !

REVERDY.

Do you wish me to hide behind a tree ?

MISS DURANT.

No, you can sit down here (indicating the bench beside her), and take my parasol — so ! — and hold it before your face, as if you were shading your eyes.

REVERDY, with the parasol.

From Miss Daisy Miller ?   It 's true she 's very dazzling ! (Daisy enters from the right, strolling slowly, as if she has nothing to do, and passes across the stage in front of the others, who sit silent, watching her, Reverdy peeping for a moment from behind his parasol. " She was dressed in white muslin, with a hundred frills and flounces, and knots of pale-colored ribbon. She was bare-headed ; but she balanced in her hand a large parasol, with a deep border of embroidery ; and she was strikingly, admirably pretty." [1]   She looks at the others as she passes them, and goes out on the left — not into the hotel. Reverdy continues.)   Now, then, may I look out ?

MISS DURANT, taking back her parasol.

She saw you, I 'm happy to say.

REVERDY.

Oh yes, I gave her a wink !

MRS. COSTELLO.

That 's the way she roams about —

---

[1] From the story.

MISS DURANT.

Seeking whom she may devour!

REVERDY.

Poor little creature! I'm the only tolerably good-looking young man in the hotel.

MRS. COSTELLO.

Mercy on us! I hope she won't get hold of Frederick!

REVERDY.

Not if I can help it, dear Madam. I have never seen Frederick — but I mistrust Frederick.

MRS. COSTELLO.

He's not at all in your style. He's had a foreign education. He speaks a dozen languages.

REVERDY, aside.

An awful prig — I can see that.

MRS. COSTELLO.

Let us hope that, thanks to his foreign education, he will be out of danger. Such people as that can only disgust him.

REVERDY.

I know the style of fellow you mean — a very high collar and a very stiff spine! He speaks a dozen languages — but he does n't speak the language of Schenectady. He won't understand an American girl — he had better leave her alone.

MISS DURANT.

I am very much obliged to you — for me!

Enter a waiter from the hotel.

REVERDY.

Oh, you are not an American; you 're an angel!

THE WAITER, approaching with a bow.

The breakfast that Madame ordered is served.

MRS. COSTELLO, to her companions.

It's just twelve o'clock; we certainly can't wait any longer.

MISS DURANT.

I don't believe he's coming at all!

MRS. COSTELLO.

Ah, if I've only brought on a headache for nothing!

REVERDY, aside.

Won't he catch it when he arrives? (They pass into the hotel, the waiter leading the way.)

SCENE THIRD.

EUGENIO, THEN WINTERBOURNE AND THE WAITER.

Eugenio comes out of the hotel, then looks about him and begins to call. He is without his hat and satchel.

EUGENIO.

Meester Randolph! Meester Randolph! Confound that infernal child — it's the fifth time this morning that I've chased him round the garden! (Stands calling again.) Meester Randolph! Meester Randolph! He is always there when he's not wanted and never when he is, and when I find him I haven't even the right to pinch his ear! He begins to kick like a little mule, and he has nails in his boots — for the mountains. Meester Randolph! Meester Randolph! Drat the little wretch — I'm a courier, not a nurse! (Exit to the right, while Winterbourne comes down from the hotel, followed by a waiter, the same who has just appeared, carrying a little tray with a service of black coffee.)

WINTERBOURNE.

I will have my coffee here, it's so close in the hotel. (The waiter places the tray on a small table, which he draws up to a bench. Winterbourne takes out a card, on which, on his pocket-book, he writes a few words.)

And please to take that card to the lady whose name I have
written there, and ask her when it will be convenient for her
to see me.

THE WAITER, looking at the card.

The Russian lady who arrived three days ago? I will let
you know, sir.

WINTERBOURNE, seated at the little table.

Wait a moment. Do you know whether Mrs. Costello
has breakfasted?

THE WAITER.

Mrs. Costello? The lady with the young lady, and the
gentleman also young?

WINTERBOURNE.

I know nothing about her companions. A lady with her
hair very high. She is rather — rather —

THE WAITER.

Yes, sir, she is rather high altogether! When she gives
an order —

WINTERBOURNE, pouring out his coffee.

I don't ask you to describe her — I ask you if she has
breakfasted.

THE WAITER.

The party 's at table now, sir. I conducted them myself,
five minutes ago. I think they waited for you, sir; they
expected you to arrive.

WINTERBOURNE.

I arrived an hour ago, by the train; but I was dusty, and
I had to have a bath. (Lighting a cigarette.) Then while I
dressed, to save time, I had my breakfast brought to my
room. Where do they usually take their coffee?

THE WAITER.

They take it in our beautiful garden, sir.

WINTERBOURNE.

Very good. I will wait for them here. That's all. (The waiter reënters the hotel. Winterbourne puffs his cigarette.) There is no use in being in a hurry. I want to be eager — but I don't want to be too eager. That worthy man is quite right; when Aunt Louisa gives an order, it's a military command. She has ordered me up from Geneva, and I've marched at the word; but I'll rest a little before reporting at head-quarters. (Puffs his cigarette.) It coincides very happily, for I don't know that, without this pretext, I should have ventured to come. Three days ago, the waiter said? A week ago, at the villa, they told me she had gone. There is always a mystery in that woman's movements. Yes, Aunt Louisa is rather high; but it's not of her I'm afraid! (Puffs a moment in silence.)

SCENE FOURTH.

WINTERBOURNE, RANDOLPH, THEN DAISY.

RANDOLPH.   He comes in from the back, approaches Winterbourne, and stops. "The child, who was diminutive for his years, had an aged expression of countenance, a pale complexion, and sharp little features. He was dressed in knickerbockers, with red stockings, which displayed his poor little spindle-shanks; he also wore a brilliant red cravat. He carried in his hand a long alpenstock, the sharp point of which he thrust into everything that he approached—the flower-beds, the garden-benches. . . . In front of Winterbourne he paused, looking at him with a pair of bright, penetrating little eyes." [1]
Winterbourne, smoking, returns his gaze.

Will you give me a lump of sugar?

WINTERBOURNE.

Yes, you may take one; but I don't think sugar is good for little boys.

[1] From the story.

RANDOLPH.   *He steps forward and carefully possesses himself of the whole contents of the plate. From these he still more carefully selects the largest lump, depositing the others in his pocket. Biting, with a grimace.*

Oh, blazes! it's hard!

WINTERBOURNE.

Take care, young man.   You'll hurt your teeth.

RANDOLPH.

I have n't got any teeth to hurt; they 've all come out. I 've only got seven teeth.   Mother counted them last night, and one came out afterwards.   She said she 'd slap me if any more came out.   I can't help it — it 's this old Europe. It 's the climate that makes 'em come out.   In America they did n't come out; it 's these hotels!

WINTERBOURNE.

If you eat all that sugar, your mother will certainly slap you.

RANDOLPH.

She 's got to give me some candy, then.   I can't get any candy here — any American candy.   American candy 's the best.

WINTERBOURNE.

And are American boys the best little boys?

RANDOLPH.

I don't know.   I 'm an American boy!

WINTERBOURNE.

I see you are one of the best.

RANDOLPH.

That is n't what my mother says, you can bet your life on that!

WINTERBOURNE.

Oh, your mother 's too modest!

RANDOLPH, astride his alpenstock, looking at Winterbourne.

She's sick — she's always sick.   It's this old Europe!
Are you an American man?

WINTERBOURNE.

Oh, yes, a fellow-citizen.   (Aside.)   I wonder whether I
was once like that!

RANDOLPH.

American men are the best.

WINTERBOURNE.

So they often say.

RANDOLPH, looking off to the left.

Here comes my sister.   She's an American girl.

WINTERBOURNE.

American girls are the best girls.

RANDOLPH.

Oh, my sister ain't the best.   She's always blowing at me!

WINTERBOURNE.

I imagine that's your fault, not hers.   (Daisy comes in from
the left in the same manner as on her previous entrance, and on reaching the middle of the stage stops and looks at Winterbourne and at Randolph, who has
converted his alpenstock into a vaulting-pole, and is springing about violently.
Winterbourne continues, getting up.)   By Jove, how pretty!

DAISY.

Well, Randolph, what *are* you doing?

RANDOLPH.

I'm going up the Alps.   This is the way!

WINTERBOURNE.

That's the way they come down.

RANDOLPH.

He's all right; he's an American man!

WINTERBOURNE, aside.

It seems to me that I have been in a manner presented. (Approaches Daisy, throwing away his cigarette. Aloud, with great civility.) This little boy and I have made acquaintance.

DAISY.   She looks at him a moment serenely, and then, as if she had scarcely heard him, addresses Randolph again.

I should like to know where you got that pole!

RANDOLPH.

The same way as you get your things.   I made Eugenio buy it.

WINTERBOURNE, aside.

With a little commission!

DAISY.

You don't mean to say you 're going to take that pole to Italy?

WINTERBOURNE, same manner.

Are you thinking of going to Italy?

DAISY, looking at him, and then looking away.

Yes, sir.

WINTERBOURNE.

Are you going over the Simplon?

DAISY.

I don't know — I suppose it 's some mountain.   Randolph, what mountain are we going over?

RANDOLPH.

Going where?

DAISY.

To Italy.   (Arranging her ribbons.)   Don't you know about Italy?

RANDOLPH.

No, and I don't want to.   I want to go to America!

WINTERBOURNE.

Oh, Italy 's a beautiful place.

RANDOLPH.

Can you get any candy there?

DAISY.

I hope not! I guess you have had candy enough, and mother thinks so too.

RANDOLPH, still jumping about.

I have n't had any for ever so long — for a hundred weeks!

DAISY.

Why, Randolph, I don't see how you can tell — (She pauses a moment.) Well I don't care! (Looks down at her dress, and continues to smooth her ribbons.)

WINTERBOURNE, aside.

Does she accept my acquaintance or not? It 's rather sudden, and it would n't do at Geneva. But why else did she come and plant herself in front of me? She is the prettiest of the pretty, and, I declare, I 'll risk it! (After a moment, aloud.) We are very fortunate in our weather, are we not?

DAISY.

Well, yes, we 've got nice weather.

WINTERBOURNE.

And still more fortunate in our scenery. (Indicating the view.)

DAISY.

Well, yes, the scenery 's lovely. It seems very mountainous.

WINTERBOURNE.

Ah, Switzerland *is* mountainous, you know.

DAISY.

I don't know much about it. We have only been here a week.

3

WINTERBOURNE, smiling.

In a week one can see a good deal.

DAISY.

Well, *we* have n't; we have only walked round a little.

WINTERBOURNE, aside.

What a remarkable type! (Aloud.) You must be rather tired : there are plenty of chairs. (Draws forward two of them.)

DAISY, looking at them a moment.

You 'll be very clever if you can get Randolph to sit.

WINTERBOURNE.

I don't care a fig about Randolph. (Daisy seats herself. Aside.) Oh, Geneva, Geneva!

DAISY, smoothing her ribbons.

Well, he 's only nine. We 've sat round a good deal, too.

WINTERBOURNE, seated beside her.

It 's very pleasant, these summer days.

DAISY.

Well, yes, it 's very pleasant. But it 's nicer in the evening.

WINTERBOURNE.

Ah, much nicer in the evening. It 's remarkably nice in the evening. (Aside.) What the deuce is she coming to ? (Aloud.) When you get to Italy you 'll find the evenings there! . . .

DAISY.

I 've heard a good deal about the evenings there.

WINTERBOURNE.

In Venice, you know — on the water — with music!

DAISY.

I don't know much about it. (With a little laugh.) I don't know much about anything!

WINTERBOURNE, aside.

Heaven forgive her, she 's charming!   I must really ascertain . . . (To Randolph, who has continued to roam about, and who comes back to them with his alpenstock, catching him and drawing him between his knees.)   Tell me your name, my beautiful boy!

RANDOLPH, struggling.

Well, you drop me first!

DAISY.

Why, Randolph, I should think you 'd like it!

WINTERBOURNE, aside.

Jupiter, that is a little strong!

RANDOLPH, liberating himself.

Try it yourself!   My name is Randolph C. Miller.

WINTERBOURNE, aside.

Alarming child!   But she does n't seem to be alarmed.

RANDOLPH, levelling his alpenstock at Daisy, who averts it with her hand.

And I 'll tell you *her* name.

DAISY, leaning back serenely.

You had better wait till you are asked.

WINTERBOURNE.

I should like very much to know your name.

RANDOLPH.

Her name is Daisy Miller.

WINTERBOURNE, expressively.

How very interesting!

DAISY, looking at him, aside.

Well, he 's a queer specimen!   I guess he 's laughing.

RANDOLPH.

That is n't her real name — that is n't her name on her cards.

DAISY.

It 's a pity that you have n't got one of my cards !

RANDOLPH.

Her name is Annie P. Miller.

WINTERBOURNE.

Oh, I see. (Aside.) That does n't tell me much.

DAISY, indicating Winterbourne.

Ask him *his* name.

RANDOLPH.

Ask him yourself ! My father's name is Ezra B. Miller. My father ain't in Europe. My father 's in a better place than Europe.

WINTERBOURNE, uncertain.

Ah, you have had the misfortune . . .

RANDOLPH.

My father 's in Schenectady. He does a big business. He 's rich, you can bet your head !

WINTERBOURNE, aside.

Oh, in Schenectady ?   I thought he meant in Paradise !

DAISY, to Randolph.

Well, you need n't stick your pole into my eye !

RANDOLPH, to Winterbourne.

Did n't I tell you she was always blowing ? (Scampers away and disappears.)

DAISY, looking after him.

He does n't like Europe ; he wants to go back. He has n't got any boys here. There 's one boy here, but he 's always going round with a teacher.

WINTERBOURNE.

And your brother has n't any teacher ?

DAISY.

Mother thought of getting him one, to travel round with us. But Randolph said he did n't want a teacher when school did n't keep; he said he would n't have lessons when he was in the cars. And we *are* in the cars most of the time. There was an English lady we met in the cars; her name was Miss Featherstone — perhaps you know her. She wanted to know why I did n't give Randolph lessons — give him instruction, she called it. I guess he could give me more instruction than I could give him! He 's very smart — he 's only nine.

WINTERBOURNE, aside.

He might be ninety!

DAISY.

Mother 's going to get a teacher for him as soon as we get to Italy. Can you get good teachers in Italy?

WINTERBOURNE.

Oh, it 's the land of art — of science.

DAISY.

Well, I guess he does n't want to study art; but she 's going to find some school, if she can. (Pensively.) Randolph ought to learn some more.

WINTERBOURNE.

It depends upon what it is!

DAISY, after a silence, during which her eyes have rested upon him.

I presume you are a German.

WINTERBOURNE, rising quickly.

Oh dear, no! I should n't have ventured to speak to you, if your brother's mention of my nationality had not seemed a guarantee . . .

DAISY, getting up.

I did n't suppose my brother knew. And you *do* speak queerly, any way!

WINTERBOURNE.

I 'm a countryman of your own. But I should tell you that I have spent many years in this old Europe, as your brother says.

DAISY.

Do you live here — in the mountains?

WINTERBOURNE, aside.

Does she think I 'm a goatherd? (Aloud.) No, I live just now at Geneva.

DAISY.

Well, you *are* peculiar, anyhow!

WINTERBOURNE, aside.

So are you, if you come to that. (Aloud.) I 'm afraid I have got rather out of the way — (pauses for a moment.)

DAISY.

Out of the way of what?

WINTERBOURNE.

Of making myself agreeable to the young ladies.

DAISY.

Have n't they got any over here? I must say I have n't seen any! Of course I have n't looked out much for them.

WINTERBOURNE.

You have looked out more for the gentlemen!

DAISY.

Well, at Schenectady I did n't have to look out.

WINTERBOURNE, aside.

Queer place, Schenectady.

DAISY.

I had so much society.   But over here — (She hesitates.)

WINTERBOURNE.

Over here ?

DAISY.

Well, you 're the first gentleman that has been at all attentive.

WINTERBOURNE.

Ah, you see, they 're afraid !

DAISY, continuing.

And the first I 've cared anything about !

WINTERBOURNE, aside.

And to think that, at the beginning, I was afraid.   (Aloud.) If they knew how kind you are they would be much less timid.

DAISY.

I hate gentlemen to be timid.   That 's only for us.

WINTERBOURNE, aside.

"For us" is enchanting !

SCENE FIFTH.

DAISY, WINTERBOURNE, EUGENIO, who comes in hastily from the right, wiping his forehead.

EUGENIO.

Mademoiselle, I have been looking for an hour for Meester Randolph.   He must be drowned in the lake !

DAISY.

I guess he 's talking to that waiter.   (Serenely.)   He likes to talk to that waiter.

EUGENIO.

He should n't talk to waiters, Mademoiselle.

WINTERBOURNE, aside.

Only to couriers — the hierarchy!

DAISY.

I want to introduce you to a friend of mine — Mr. — Mr. — (To Winterbourne.) I declare, I don't know your name.

WINTERBOURNE, aside.

To the courier? Excuse me!

EUGENIO, very proper.

I have the honor of knowing the name of Monsieur.

DAISY.

Gracious, you know everything!

EUGENIO, aside.

The lover of the Katkoff! (Aloud.) I found Meester Randolph, but he escaped again.

DAISY.

Well, Eugenio, you 're a splendid courier, but you can't make much impression on Randolph.

EUGENIO.

I do what I can, Mademoiselle. The lunch is waiting, and Madame is at the table. If you will excuse me, I will give up the chase. (Glancing at Winterbourne, aside.) Is he leaving the Katkoff for the child?

DAISY.

You need n't be so grand, need he? (To Winterbourne.) It 's not the first time you 've been introduced to a courier!

WINTERBOURNE, stiffly.

The very first.

EUGENIO, aside.

He has never kept one. (Aloud.) If Mademoiselle will pass into the hotel! (Aside again.) The child is not for every one.

DAISY.

Tell mother to begin — that I 'm talking to a gentleman.

WINTERBOURNE, protesting.

I shall be very sorry to incommode your mother.

DAISY, smiling.

I like the way you say such things. (Familiarly.) What are you going to do all day?

WINTERBOURNE, embarrassed.

I hardly know. I 've only just arrived.

DAISY.

I will come out after lunch.

WINTERBOURNE, with extreme respect.

I shall be here, to take your commands.

DAISY.

Well, you *do* say them! About two o'clock.

WINTERBOURNE.

I shall not go far.

DAISY, going.

And I shall learn your name from Eugenio.

EUGENIO, aside.

And something else as well! He is not for the child. (Follows Daisy into the hotel.)

SCENE SIXTH.

WINTERBOURNE ALONE, THEN MADAME DE KATKOFF.

WINTERBOURNE.

She's simply amazing! I have never seen them like that. I have seen them worse — oh, yes! — and I have seen them better; but I've never encountered that particular shade — that familiarity, that facility, that fragility! She's too audacious to be innocent, and too candid to be — the other thing. But her candor itself is a queer affair. Coming up to me and proposing acquaintance, and letting her eyes rest on mine! Planting herself there like a flower to be gathered! Introducing me to her courier, and offering me a rendezvous at the end of twenty minutes! Are they all like that, the little American girls? It's time I should go back and see. (Seeing Madame de Katkoff.) But I can hardly go while I have this reason for staying!

MADAME DE KATKOFF. She comes out of the hotel; she has still her book under her arm.

They brought me your card, but I thought it better I should come and see you here.

WINTERBOURNE.

I know why you do that: you think it's less encouraging than to receive me in-doors.

MADAME DE KATKOFF, smiling.

Oh, if I could discourage you a little!

WINTERBOURNE.

It's not for want of trying. I bore you so much!

MADAME DE KATKOFF.

No, you don't bore me, but you distress me. I give you so little.

WINTERBOURNE.

That's for me to measure. I'm content for the present.

MADAME DE KATKOFF.

If you had been content, you would n't have followed me to this place.

WINTERBOURNE.

I did n't follow you, and, to speak perfectly frankly, it's not for you I came.

MADAME DE KATKOFF.

Is it for that young lady I just saw from my window?

WINTERBOURNE.

I never heard of that young lady before. I came for an aunt of mine, who is staying here.

MADAME DE KATKOFF, smiling again.

Ah, if your family could only take an interest in you!

WINTERBOURNE.

Don't count on them too much. I have n't seen my aunt yet.

MADAME DE KATKOFF.

You have asked first for me? You see, then, it *was* for me you came.

WINTERBOURNE.

I wish I could believe it pleased you a little to think so.

MADAME DE KATKOFF.

It does please me— a little; I like you very much.

WINTERBOURNE.

You always say that, when you are about to make some particularly disagreeable request. You like me, but you dislike my society. On that principle, I wish you hated me!

MADAME DE KATKOFF.

I may come to it yet.

WINTERBOURNE.

Before that, then, won't you sit down ?   (Indicating a bench.)

MADAME DE KATKOFF.

Thank you ; I 'm not tired.

WINTERBOURNE.

That would be too encouraging ! I went to the villa a week ago. You had already left it.

MADAME DE KATKOFF.

I went first to Lausanne. If I had remained there, you would n't have found me.

WINTERBOURNE.

I 'm delighted you did n't remain. But I 'm sorry you are altering your house.

MADAME DE KATKOFF.

Only two rooms. That 's why I came away : the work-men made too much noise.

WINTERBOURNE.

I hope they are not the rooms I know — in which the happiest hours of my life have been passed !

MADAME DE KATKOFF.

I see why you wished me to sit down. You want to begin a siege.

WINTERBOURNE.

No, I was only going to say that I shall always see with particular vividness your little blue parlor.

MADAME DE KATKOFF.

They are going to change it to red.   (Aside.)   Perhaps that will cure him !   (Aloud.)   Apropos of your family, have they come to Europe to bring you home ?

WINTERBOURNE.

As I tell you, I have n't yet ascertained their intentions.

MADAME DE KATKOFF.

I take a great interest in them.   I feel a little responsible for you.

WINTERBOURNE.

You don't care a straw for me!

MADAME DE KATKOFF.

Let me give you a proof.   I think it would conduce to your happiness to return for a while to America.

WINTERBOURNE.

To *my* happiness?   You are confounding it with your own.

MADAME DE KATKOFF.

It is true that the two things are rather distinct.   But you have been in Europe for years — for years and years.

WINTERBOURNE.

Oh, I have been here too long.   I know that.

MADAME DE KATKOFF.

You ought to go over and make the acquaintance of your compatriots.

WINTERBOURNE.

Going over is n't necessary.   I can do it here.

MADAME DE KATKOFF.

You ought at least to see their institutions — their scenery.

WINTERBOURNE.

Don't talk about scenery, on the Lake of Geneva!   As for American institutions, I can see them in their fruits.

MADAME DE KATKOFF.

In their fruits?

WINTERBOURNE.

Little nectarines and plums.   A very pretty bloom, but decidedly crude.   What book are you reading?

MADAME DE KATKOFF.

I don't know what. The last French novel.

WINTERBOURNE.

Are you going to remain in the garden?

MADAME DE KATKOFF, looks at him a moment.

I see what you are coming to: you wish to offer to read to me.

WINTERBOURNE.

As I did in the little blue parlor!

MADAME DE KATKOFF.

You read very well; but we are not there now.

WINTERBOURNE.

A quiet corner, under the trees, will do as well.

MADAME DE KATKOFF.

We neither of us have the time. I recommend you to your aunt. She will be sure to take you in hand.

WINTERBOURNE.

I have an idea I shan't fall in love with my aunt.

MADAME DE KATKOFF.

I am sorry for her. I should like you as a nephew.

WINTERBOURNE.

I should like you as a serious woman!

MADAME DE KATKOFF.

I am intensely serious. Perhaps you will believe it when I tell you that I leave this place to-day.

WINTERBOURNE.

I don't call that serious: I call it cruel.

MADAME DE KATKOFF.

At all events, it's deliberate. Vevey is too hot; I shall go higher up into the mountains.

WINTERBOURNE.

You knew it was hot when you came.

MADAME DE KATKOFF, after a pause, with significance.

Yes, but it's hotter than I supposed.

WINTERBOURNE.

You don't like meeting old friends.

MADAME DE KATKOFF, aside.

No, nor old enemies! (Aloud.)   I like old friends in the autumn — the melancholy season!   I shall count on seeing you then.

WINTERBOURNE.

And not before, of course.   Say at once you wish to cut me.

MADAME DE KATKOFF, smiling.

Very good: I wish to cut you!

WINTERBOURNE.

You give a charm even to that!   Where shall you be in the autumn?

MADAME DE KATKOFF.

I shall be at the villa — if the little blue parlor is altered! In the winter I shall go to Rome.

WINTERBOURNE.

A happy journey, then!   I shall go to America.

MADAME DE KATKOFF.

That's capital.   Let me give you a word of advice.

WINTERBOURNE.

Yes, that's the finishing touch!

MADAME DE KATKOFF.

The little nectarines and plums: don't mind if they *are* a trifle crude!   Pick out a fair one, a sweet one —

WINTERBOURNE, stopping her with a gesture.

Don't, don't! I shall see you before you go.

MADAME DE KATKOFF, aside.

Not if I can help it! (Aloud.) I think this must be your family. (Goes into the hotel.)

SCENE SEVENTH.

WINTERBOURNE, MRS. COSTELLO, MISS DURANT, REVERDY, who come out of the hotel as Madame de Katkoff enters it.

REVERDY.

We are always meeting the Russian princess!

MISS DURANT.

If you call that meeting her, when she never looks at you!

MRS. COSTELLO.

She does n't look at you, but she sees you. Bless my soul, if here is n't Frederick!

WINTERBOURNE.

My dear aunt, I was only waiting till you had breakfasted.

MISS DURANT, aside.

He was talking with the Russian princess!

MRS. COSTELLO.

You might have sat down with us : we waited an hour.

WINTERBOURNE.

I breakfasted in my room. I was obliged on my arrival to jump into a bath.

MISS DURANT, aside.

He 's very cold — he 's very cold!

WINTERBOURNE.

They told me you were at table, and I just sat down here.

MRS. COSTELLO.

You were in no hurry to embrace me — after ten years?

WINTERBOURNE.

It was just because of those ten years; they seemed to make you so venerable that I was pausing — as at the entrance of a shrine! Besides, I knew you had charming company.

MRS. COSTELLO.

You shall discover how charming. This is Alice Durant, who is almost our cousin.

WINTERBOURNE, smiling.

Almost? I wish it were quite.

MRS. COSTELLO.

And that is Mr. Charles Reverdy.

REVERDY.

Who is almost their courier!

WINTERBOURNE.

I must relieve you of your duties.

REVERDY, aside.

Oh, thank you, thank you! By George, if I 'm relieved I 'll look out for Miss Miller. (Looks about him, and finally steals away.)

MRS. COSTELLO.

My dear Frederick, in all this time you have not changed for the worse.

WINTERBOURNE.

How can you tell that — in three minutes?

MISS DURANT, aside.

Decidedly good-looking, but fearfully distant!

MRS. COSTELLO.

Oh, if you are not agreeable, we shall be particularly disappointed. We count on you immensely.

4

WINTERBOURNE.

I shall do my best, dear aunt.

MRS. COSLELLO.

Especially for our sweet Alice.

MISS DURANT.

Oh, Cousin Louisa, how can you?

MRS. COSTELLO.

I thought of you when I invited her to come to Europe.

WINTERBOURNE.

It was a very happy thought. I don't mean thinking of me, but inviting Miss Durant.

MISS DURANT, to Winterbourne.

I can't say it was of you I thought when I accepted.

WINTERBOURNE.

I should never flatter myself : there are too many other objects of interest.

MRS. COSTELLO.

That 's precisely what we have been talking of. We are surrounded by objects of interest, and we depend upon you to be our guide.

WINTERBOURNE.

My dear aunt, I 'm afraid I don't know much about them.

MRS. COSTELLO.

You 'll have a motive to-day for learning. I have an idea that you have always wanted a motive. In that stupid old Geneva there can't be many.

WINTERBOURNE.

Ah, if there 's one, it 's enough !

MISS DURANT, aside.

If there 's *one ?* He 's in love with some dreadful Genevese !

MRS. COSTELLO.

My young companion has a great desire to ascend a mountain — to examine a glacier.

MISS DURANT.

Cousin Louisa, you make me out too bold !

WINTERBOURNE, aside.

She 's not bold, then, this one, like the other ?   I think I prefer the other. (Aloud.) You should go to Zermatt. You 're in the midst of the glaciers there.

MRS. COSTELLO.

We shall be delighted to go — under your escort. Mr. Reverdy will look after *me !*

MISS DURANT, glancing about for him.

When he has done with Miss Daisy Miller !

WINTERBOURNE, smiling.

Even among the glaciers, I flatter myself I can take care of both of you.

MISS DURANT.

It will be all the easier, as I never leave your aunt.

MRS. COSTELLO.

She does n't rush about the world alone, like so many American girls. She has been brought up like the young ladies in Geneva. Her education was surrounded with every precaution.

WINTERBOURNE, smiling.

With too many, perhaps ! The best education is seeing the world a little.

MRS. COSTELLO.

That 's precisely what I wish her to do. When we have finished Zermatt, we wish to come back to Interlaken, and from Interlaken you shall take us to Lucerne.

WINTERBOURNE, gravely.

Perhaps you 'll draw up a little list.

MISS DURANT, aside.

Perfectly polite, but no enthusiasm! (Aloud.) I 'm afraid Mr. Winterbourne is n't at liberty; he has *other* friends.

MRS. COSTELLO.

He has n't another aunt, I imagine!

WINTERBOURNE, aside.

Fortunately not! (Aloud to Miss Durant.) It 's very charming of you to think of that.

MISS DURANT.

Possibly we are indiscreet, as we just saw you talking to a lady.

WINTERBOURNE.

Madame de Katkoff? She leaves this place to-day.

MRS. COSTELLO.

You don't mean to follow her, I hope? (Aside.) It 's best to be firm with him at the start.

WINTERBOURNE.

My dear aunt, I don't follow every woman I speak to.

MISS DURANT, aside.

Ah, that 's meant for us! Mr. Reverdy is never so rude. I would thank him to come back.

MRS. COSTELLO.

On the 1st of October, you know, you shall take us to Italy.

WINTERBOURNE.

Ah! every one is going to Italy.

MISS DURANT.

Every one? Madame de Katkoff, perhaps.

WINTERBOURNE.

Madame de Katkoff, precisely; and Mr. Randolph C.
Miller and his sister Daisy.

MRS. COSTELLO.

Bless my soul!   What do you know about that?

WINTERBOURNE.

I know what they have told me.

MRS. COSTELLO.

Mercy on us!   What opportunity? —

WINTERBOURNE.

Just now, while I had my coffee.

MISS DURANT.

As I say, Mr. Winterbourne has a great many friends.

WINTERBOURNE.

He only asks to add you to the number.

MISS DURANT.

Side by side with Miss Daisy Miller?   Thank you very
much.

MRS. COSTELLO.

Come, my dear Frederick, that girl is not your friend.

WINTERBOURNE.

Upon my word, I don't know what she is, and I should
be very glad if you could tell me.

MRS. COSTELLO.

That 's very easily done: she 's a little American flirt.

WINTERBOURNE.

Ah! she 's a little American flirt!

MISS DURANT.

She 's a vulgar little chatterbox.

WINTERBOURNE.

Ah! she 's a vulgar little chatterbox!

MRS. COSTELLO.

She's in no sort of society.

WINTERBOURNE.

Ah! she's in no sort of society!

MISS DURANT.

You would never know her in America.

WINTERBOURNE.

If I should never know her in America, it seems to me a reason for seizing the opportunity here.

MRS. COSTELLO.

The opportunity appears to have come to you very easily.

WINTERBOURNE.

I confess it did, rather. We fell into conversation while I sat there on the bench.

MRS. COSTELLO.

Perhaps she sat down beside you?

WINTERBOURNE.

I won't deny that she did; she is wonderfully charming.

MISS DURANT.

Oh! if that's all that's necessary to be charming —

MRS. COSTELLO.

You must give up the attempt — must n't you, my dear? My poor Frederick, this is very dreadful!

WINTERBOURNE.

So it seems; but I don't understand.

MRS. COSTELLO.

What should you say at Geneva of a young woman who made such advances?

WINTERBOURNE.

Such advances? I don't know that they were advances.

MRS. COSTELLO.

Ah! if you wish to wait till she invites you to her room!

WINTERBOURNE, laughing.

I shall not have to wait very long.

MISS DURANT.

Had n't I better leave you?

MRS. COSTELLO.

Poor child, I understand that you shrink . . . But we must make it clear.

MISS DURANT.

Oh, yes, we must make it clear!

WINTERBOURNE.

Do make it clear; I want it to be clear.

MRS. COSTELLO.

Ask yourself, then, what they would say at Geneva.

WINTERBOURNE.

They would say she was rather far gone.   But we are not at Geneva.

MRS. COSTELLO.

We are only a few miles off.   Miss Daisy Miller is very far gone indeed.

WINTERBOURNE.

Ah! what a pity!   But I thought, now, in New York —

MRS. COSTELLO, sternly.

Frederick, don't lift your hand against your mother-country!

WINTERBOURNE.

Never in the world.   I only repeat what I hear — that over there all this sort of thing — the manners of young persons, the standard of propriety — is quite different.

MISS DURANT.

I only know how *I* was brought up!

WINTERBOURNE, slightly ironical.

Ah, that settles it.

MRS. COSTELLO.

We must take him back with us, to see.

WINTERBOURNE.

Not to see, you mean — not to see my dear little friend !

MRS. COSTELLO.

In the best society — never.

WINTERBOURNE.

Oh, hang the best society, then !

MRS. COSTELLO, with majesty.

I am exceedingly obliged to you.

WINTERBOURNE.

Oh, *you* are the best society ! And the little girl with the naughty brother is the worst ?

MRS. COSTELLO.

The worst *I* have ever seen.

WINTERBOURNE, rather gravely, laying his hand on her arm.

My dear aunt, the best, then, ought to be awfully good !

MISS DURANT, aside.

He means that for an epigram ! I 'll make him go and look for Mr. Reverdy. (Aloud.) I wonder what has become of Mr. Reverdy.

MRS. COSTELLO, sharply.

Never mind Mr. Reverdy; I 'll look after him. (To Winterbourne.) If you should see a little more of those vulgar people, you would find that they don't stand the test.

WINTERBOURNE.

Oh, I shall see a little more of them — in a quarter of an hour. (Looking at his watch.) The young lady is coming back at two o'clock.

MRS. COSTELLO.

Gracious goodness! Have you made an appointment?

WINTERBOURNE.

I don't know whether it's an appointment, but she said she would come back again.

MRS. COSTELLO, to Miss Durant.

My precious darling, *we* must go in. We can hardly be expected to assist at such a scene.

WINTERBOURNE.

My dear aunt, there is plenty of time yet.

MISS DURANT.

Ah, no ; she 'll be before ! Would you kindly look for Mr. Reverdy ?

WINTERBOURNE, extremely polite.

With the greatest of pleasure.

MRS. COSTELLO.

Later in the afternoon, if this extraordinary interview is over, we should like you to go with us into the town.

WINTERBOURNE, in the same tone.

With the greatest of pleasure. (Aside.) They hate her ferociously, and it makes me feel sorry for her.

MRS. COSTELLO, to Miss Durant.

Quickly, my dear ! We must get out of the way.

WINTERBOURNE.

Let me at least see you into the house. (Accompanies them into the hotel.)

SCENE EIGHTH.

CHARLES REVERDY, RANDOLPH, then DAISY.

REVERDY, coming in from behind with the child on his back.

The horrid little wretch! I'm like Sinbad the Sailor with the Old Man of the Sea! Don't you think you've had about enough?

RANDOLPH, snapping a little whip.

Oh, no; I have n't had enough. I'll tell you when I've had enough.

REVERDY.

Oh, come! I've galloped twenty miles; I've been through all my paces. You must sit still in the saddle a while. (Pauses in front while Randolph bounces up and down.) I'm playing horse with the brother to be agreeable to the sister; but he's riding me to death!

RANDOLPH, still brandishing his whip.

I want you to prance about and to kick. Get up, sir; get up!

REVERDY, aside.

It's the devil's own game — here at the door of the hotel! (Aloud.) I'll prance about so that you'll come off.

RANDOLPH, firm in his place.

If you throw me off, I'll give you a licking! Get up, sir, get up!

REVERDY, aside.

Damn the little demon! It was a happy thought of mine.

RANDOLPH, kicking.

These are my spurs. I'll drive in my spurs! Get up, sir, get up!

REVERDY.

Oh misery, here goes! (He begins to imitate the curvetting of a horse, in the hope of throwing Randolph off, but, seeing Daisy issue from the hotel, suddenly stops.)

DAISY, staring.

Well, Randolph, what are you doing up there?

RANDOLPH.

I'm riding on a mule!

REVERDY, with a groan.

A mule? Not even the nobler animal! My dear young lady, could n't you persuade him to dismount?

DAISY, laughing.

You look so funny when you say that! I'm sure I never persuaded Randolph.

RANDOLPH.

He said if I would tell him where you were, he would give me a ride.

REVERDY.

And then, when he was up, he refused to tell me!

RANDOLPH.

I told you mother would n't like it. She wants Daisy and me to be proper.

REVERDY, aside.

"Me to be proper!" He 's really sublime, the little fiend!

DAISY.

Well, she does want you to be proper. She 's waiting for you at lunch.

RANDOLPH.

I don't want any lunch: there 's nothing fit to eat.

DAISY.

Well, I guess there is, if you 'll go and see.

REVERDY, aside.

It 's uncommonly nice for me, while they argue the question !

DAISY.

There 's a man with candy in the hall; that 's where mother wants you to be proper.

RANDOLPH, jumping down.

A man with candy.   Oh, blazes !

REVERDY, aside.

Adorable creature !   She has broken the spell.

RANDOLPH, scampering into the hotel.

I say, old mule, you can go to grass !

REVERDY.

Delightful little nature, your brother.

DAISY.

Well, he used to have a pony at home.   I guess he misses that pony.   Is it true that you asked him that ?

REVERDY.

To tell me where you were ?   I confess I wanted very much to know.

DAISY.

Well, Randolph could n't tell you.   I was having lunch with mother.   I thought you were with those ladies.

REVERDY.

Whom you saw me with this morning ?   Oh, no ; they 've got another cavalier, just arrived, on purpose.

DAISY, attentive.

Another cavalier — just arrived ?   Do you mean that gentleman that speaks so beautifully ?

REVERDY.

A dozen languages ?   His English is n't bad — compared with my French !

DAISY, thoughtful.

Well, he looks like a cavalier. Did he come on purpose for them?

REVERDY, aside.

What does she know about him? (Aloud.) Oh, yes; they sent for him to Geneva.

DAISY.

To Geneva? That's the one!

REVERDY.

You see, they want him to be always with them; he's for their own particular consumption.

DAISY, disappointed, but very simply.

Ah, then he won't come out at two o'clock!

REVERDY.

I'm sure I don't know. (The bell of the hotel strikes two.) There it is. You'll have a chance to see. (Winterbourne, on the stroke of the hour, comes out of the hotel.)

DAISY, joyfully.

Here he comes! He's too sweet!

REVERDY, aside.

Oh, I say, she had made an appointment with him while I was doing the mule!

SCENE NINTH.

REVERDY, FOR A MOMENT; DAISY, WINTERBOURNE.

WINTERBOURNE, to Reverdy.

I am glad to find you: Miss Durant has a particular desire to see you.

REVERDY.

It's very good of you to be her messenger. (Aside.) That's what he calls relieving me!

WINTERBOURNE.

You will find those ladies in their own sitting-room, on the second floor.

REVERDY.

Oh, I know where it is. (To Daisy.) I shall be back in five minutes.

DAISY.

I 'm sure you need n't hurry.

WINTERBOURNE.

I have an idea they have a good deal to say to you.

REVERDY.

I hope it is n't to complain of you! (Goes into the hotel.)

DAISY, looking at Winterbourne a moment.

I was afraid you would n't come.

WINTERBOURNE, aside.

She has a way of looking at you! (Aloud.) I don't know what can have given you such an impression.

DAISY.

Well, you know, half the time they don't — the gentlemen.

WINTERBOURNE.

That 's in America, perhaps. But over here they always come.

DAISY, simply.

Well, I have n't had much experience over here.

WINTERBOURNE.

I am glad to hear it. It was very good of your mother to let you leave her again.

DAISY, surprised.

Oh, mother does n't care; she has got Eugenio.

WINTERBOURNE, startled.

Surely, not to sit with her?

DAISY.

Well, he does n't sit with her always, because he likes to go out.

WINTERBOURNE.

Oh, he likes to go out!

DAISY.

He 's got a great many friends, Eugenio; he 's awfully popular. And then, you know, poor mother is n't very amusing.

WINTERBOURNE.

Ah, she is n't very amusing! (Aside.) Aunt Louisa was right: it is n't the best society!

DAISY.

But Eugenio stays with her all he can: he says he did n't expect that so much when he came.

WINTERBOURNE.

I should think not! I hope at least that it is n't a monopoly, and that I may have the pleasure of making your mother's acquaintance.

DAISY.

Well, you *do* speak beautifully! I told Mr. Reverdy.

WINTERBOURNE.

It was very good of you to mention it. One speaks as one can.

DAISY.

Mother 's awfully timid, or else I 'd introduce you. She always makes a fuss if I introduce a gentleman. But I do introduce them — the ones I like.

WINTERBOURNE.

If it 's a sign of your liking, I hope you will introduce me. But you must know my name, which you did n't a while ago.

DAISY.

Oh, Eugenio has told me your name, and I think it 's very pretty.   And he has told me something else.

WINTERBOURNE.

I can't imagine what he should tell you about me.

DAISY.

About you and some one else — that Russian lady who is leaving the hotel.

WINTERBOURNE, quickly.

Who is leaving the hotel !   How does he know that ?

DAISY, with a little laugh.

You see it *is* true : you are very fond of that Russian lady !

WINTERBOURNE, aside.

She is leaving the hotel — but not till six o'clock.   (Aloud.) I have n't known you very long, but I should like to give you a piece of advice.   Don't gossip with your courier !

DAISY.

I see you 're offended — and it proves Eugenio was right. He said it was a secret — and you don't like me to know it.

WINTERBOURNE.

You may know everything, my dear young lady ; only don't get your information from a servant.

DAISY.

Do you call Eugenio a servant ?   He 'll be amused if I tell him that !

WINTERBOURNE.

He won't be amused — he will be furious ; but the particular emotion does n't matter.   It 's very good of you to take such an interest.

DAISY.

Oh, I don't know what I should do if I did n't take some interest! You do care for her, then?

WINTERBOURNE, a little annoyed.

For the Russian lady? Oh, yes, we are old friends. (Aside.) My aunt 's right: they don't stand the test!

DAISY.

I 'm very glad she is going, then. But the others mean to stay?

WINTERBOURNE.

The others? What others?

DAISY.

The two that Mr. Reverdy told me about, and to whom he 's so very devoted.

WINTERBOURNE.

It 's my aunt and a friend of hers; but you need n't mind them.

DAISY.

For all they mind me! But they look very stylish.

WINTERBOURNE.

Oh, yes, they are very stylish; you can bet your life on that, as your brother says!

DAISY, looking at him a moment.

Did you come for them, or for the Russian lady?

WINTERBOURNE, aside, more annoyed.

Ah, too many questions! (Aloud.) I came for none of them; I came for myself.

DAISY, serenely.

Yes, that 's the impression you give me: you think a great deal of yourself! But I should like to know your aunt, all the same. She has her hair done like an old picture, and she holds herself so very well; she speaks to no one, and she dines in private. That's the way I should like to be!

WINTERBOURNE.

Ah, you would make a bad exchange. My aunt is liable to fearful headaches.

DAISY.

I think she is very elegant — headaches and all! I want very much to know her.

WINTERBOURNE, aside.

Goodness, what a happy thought! (Aloud.) She would be enchanted; only the state of her health . . .

DAISY.

Oh, yes, she has an excuse; that's a part of the elegance! I should like to have an excuse. Any one can see your aunt would have one.

WINTERBOURNE.

Oh, she has five hundred!

DAISY.

Well, *we* have n't any, mother and I. I like a lady to be exclusive. I 'm dying to be exclusive myself.

WINTERBOURNE.

Be just as you are. You would n't be half so charming if you were different. (Aside.) It 's odd how true that is, with all her faults!

DAISY.

You don't think me charming : you only think me queer. I can see that by your manner. I should like to know your aunt, any way.

WINTERBOURNE.

It 's very good of you, I 'm sure; but I am afraid those headaches will interfere.

DAISY.

I suppose she does n't have a headache every day, does she?

WINTERBOURNE, aside.

What the deuce is a man to say? (Aloud.) She assures me she does.

DAISY, turns away a moment, walks to the parapet, and stands there thoughtful.

She does n't want to know me! (Looking at Winterbourne.) Why don't you say so? You need n't be afraid; I 'm not afraid. (Suddenly, with a little break in her voice.) Gracious, she *is* exclusive!

WINTERBOURNE.

So much the worse for her!

DAISY.

You see, you 've got to own to it! Well, I don't care. I mean to be like that — when I 'm old.

WINTERBOURNE.

I can't think you 'll ever be old.

DAISY.

Oh, you horrid thing! As if I were going to perish in my flower!

WINTERBOURNE.

I should be very sorry if I thought that. But you will never have any quarrel with Time : he 'll touch you very gently.

DAISY, at the parapet, looking over the lake.

I hope I shall never have any quarrel with any one. I 'm very good-natured.

WINTERBOURNE, laughing.

You certainly disarm criticism — oh, completely!

DAISY.

Well, I don't care. Have you ever been to that old cas-tle? (Pointing to Chillon, in the distance.)

WINTERBOURNE.

The Castle of Chillon? Yes, in former days, more than once. I suppose you have been there, too.

DAISY.

Oh, no, we have n't been there. I want to go there awfully. Of course, I mean to go there. I would n't go away from here without having seen that old castle!

WINTERBOURNE.

It 's a very pretty excursion, and very easy to make. You can drive, you know, or you can take the little steamer.

DAISY.

Well, we were going last week, but mother gave out. She suffers terribly from dyspepsia. She said she could n't go. Randolph won't go, either: he does n't think much of old castles.

WINTERBOURNE, smiling.

Ah, your brother is n't interested in historical monuments?

DAISY.

Well, he 's generally disappointed. He wants to stay round here. Mother 's afraid to leave him alone, and Eugenio can't be induced to stay with him, so that we have n't been to many places. But it will be too bad if we don't go up to that castle.

WINTERBOURNE.

I think it might be arranged. Let me see. Could n't you get some one to remain for the afternoon with Randolph?

DAISY, suddenly.

Oh, yes; we could get Mr. Reverdy!

WINTERBOURNE.

Mr. Reverdy?

DAISY.

He's awfully fond of Randolph; they're always fooling round.

WINTERBOURNE, laughing.

It is n't a bad idea.   Reverdy must lay in a stock of sugar.

DAISY.

There's one thing : with you, mother will be afraid to go.

WINTERBOURNE.

She carries her timidity too far !   We must wait till she has got used to me.

DAISY.

I don't want to wait.   I want to go right off.

WINTERBOURNE.

Ah, you can hardly force her to come, you know.

DAISY.

I don't want to force her : I want to leave her !

WINTERBOURNE.

To leave her behind ?   What, then, would you do for an escort ?

DAISY, serenely.

I would take you.

WINTERBOURNE, astounded.

Me ?   Me alone?

DAISY, laughing.

You seem about as timid as mother !   Never mind, I 'll take care of you.

WINTERBOURNE, still bewildered.

Off to Chillon — with you alone — right off ?

DAISY, eagerly questioning.

Right off ?   Could we go now ?

WINTERBOURNE, aside.

She takes away my breath !   (Aloud.)   There's a boat just after three.

DAISY.

We'll go straight on board !

WINTERBOURNE, aside.

She has known me for a couple of hours !   (Aloud, rather formally.)   The privilege for me is immense ; but I feel as if I ought to urge you to reflect a little.

DAISY.

So as to show how stiff you can be ?   Oh, I know all about that.

WINTERBOURNE.

No, just to remind you that your mother will certainly discover . . .

DAISY, staring.

Will certainly discover?

WINTERBOURNE.

Your little escapade.   You can't hide it.

DAISY, amazed, and a little touched.

I don't know what you mean.   I have nothing to hide.

WINTERBOURNE, aside.

Ah, I give it up !   (Seeing Eugenio, who comes out of the hotel.) And here comes that odious creature, to spoil it !

SCENE TENTH.

WINTERBOURNE, DAISY, EUGENIO.

EUGENIO.

Mademoiselle, your mother requests that you will come to her.

DAISY.

I don't believe a word of it !

EUGENIO.

You should not do me the injustice to doubt of my honor!
Madame asked me to look for you ten minutes ago; but I
was detained by meeting in the hall a lady (speaking slowly, and
looking at Winterbourne), a Russian lady, whom I once had the
honor to serve, and who was leaving the hotel.

WINTERBOURNE, startled, aside.

Madame de Katkoff — leaving already?

EUGENIO, watching Winterbourne.

She had so many little bags that she could hardly settle
herself in the carriage, and I thought it my duty — I have
had so much practice — to show her how to stow them
away.

WINTERBOURNE, quickly, to Daisy.

Will you kindly excuse me a moment?

EUGENIO, obsequious, interposing.

If it's to overtake the Russian lady, Madame de Katkoff
is already far away.   (Aside.)   She had four horses: I
frightened her more than a little!

WINTERBOURNE, aside.

Far away — without another word?   She can be hard —
when she tries. Very good. Let me see if I can be the
same!

DAISY, noticing Winterbourne, aside.

Poor man, he's stiffer than ever!   But I'm glad she
has gone.   (Aloud.)   See here, Eugenio, I'm going to that
castle.

EUGENIO, with a certain impertinence.

Mademoiselle has made arrangements?

DAISY.

Well, if Mr. Winterbourne does n't back out.

WINTERBOURNE.

Back out? I sha'n't be happy till we are off! (Aside.) I'll go anywhere — with any one — *now ;* and if the poor girl is injured by it, it is n't my fault!

EUGENIO.

I think Mademoiselle will find that Madame is in no state —

DAISY.

My dear Eugenio, Madame will stay at home with you.

WINTERBOURNE, wincing, aside.

If she would only not call him her " dear " !

EUGENIO.

I take the liberty of advising Mademoiselle not to go to the castle.

WINTERBOURNE, irritated.

You had better remember that your place is not to advise, but to look after the little bags !

DAISY.

Oh, I hoped you would make a fuss ! But I don't want to go now.

WINTERBOURNE, decided.

I shall make a fuss if you don't go.

DAISY, nervously, with a little laugh.

That 's all I want — a little fuss !

WINTERBOURNE, aside.

She 's not so easy as she would like to appear. She knows it 's a risk — but she likes the risk.

EUGENIO.

If Mademoiselle will come with me, I will undertake to organize a fuss. (A steamboat whistle is heard in the distance.)

WINTERBOURNE, to Daisy.

The boat's coming up.　You have only till three o'clock.

DAISY, suddenly decided.

Oh, I can be quick when I try !　(Hurries into the hotel.)

WINTERBOURNE, looking a moment at Eugenio.

You had better not interfere with that young lady !

EUGENIO, insolent.

I suppose you mean that I had better not interfere with
you !　You had better not defy me to do so !　(Aside.)　It's
a pity I sent away the Katkoff !　(Follows Daisy into the hotel.)

WINTERBOURNE, alone.

That's a singularly offensive beast !　And what the mis-
chief does he mean by his having been in *her* service ?
Thank heaven she has got rid of him !　(Seeing Mrs. Costello, Miss
Durant, and Charles Reverdy, who issue from the hotel, the ladies dressed for a
walk.)　Oh, confusion, I had forgotten *them !*

SCENE ELEVENTH.

MRS.　COSTELLO, MISS DURANT, CHARLES REVERDY,
WINTERBOURNE, then DAISY.

MRS. COSTELLO.

Well, Frederick, we take for granted that your little interview is over, and that you are ready to accompany us into
the town.

WINTERBOURNE.

Over, dear aunt ?　Why, it's only just begun.　We are
going to the Château de Chillon.

MRS. COSTELLO.

You and that little girl?　You will hardly get us to believe
that !

REVERDY, *aside, still with the camp-stool.*

Hang me, why did n't I think of that?

WINTERBOURNE.

I am afraid I rather incommode you; but I shall be delighted to go into the town when we come back.

MISS DURANT.

You had better never come back.   No one will speak to you!

MRS. COSTELLO.

My dear Frederick, if you are joking, your joke is in dreadful taste.

WINTERBOURNE.

I am not joking, in the least.   The young lady is to be here at three.

MRS. COSTELLO.

She herself is joking, then.   She won't be so crazy as to come.

REVERDY, *who has gone to the parapet and looked off to right, coming back, taking out his watch.*

It 's close upon three, and the boat 's at the wharf.

WINTERBOURNE, *watch in hand.*

Not quite yet.   Give her a moment's grace.

MRS. COSTELLO.

It won't be for us to give her grace : it will be for society.

WINTERBOURNE.

Ah, but you *are* society, you know.   She wants immensely to know you.

MRS. COSTELLO.

Is that why she is flinging herself at *you?*

WINTERBOURNE, *very gravely.*

Listen to me seriously, please.   The poor little girl has given me a great mark — a very touching mark — of confidence. I wish to present her to you, because I wish some one to answer for my honor.

MRS. COSTELLO.

And pray, who is to answer for hers?

WINTERBOURNE.

Oh, I say, you 're cruel!

MRS. COSTELLO.

I am an old woman, Frederick; but I thank my stars I am not too old to be horrified! (The bell of the steamboat is heard to ring in the distance.)

REVERDY.

There 's your boat, sir. I 'm afraid you 'll miss it!

WINTERBOURNE, watch still in hand, aside.

Three o'clock. Damn that courier!

MRS. COSTELLO.

If she does n't come, you may present her.

MISS DURANT.

She won't come. We must do her justice.

DAISY, hurrying out of the hotel.

I say, Mr. Winterbourne, I 'm as punctual as you! (She wears a charming travelling-dress, and is buttoning her glove. Eugenio appears in the porch of the hotel, and stands there, with his hands in his pockets, and with a baffled but vindictive air, watching the rest of the scene.)

REVERDY.

Alas, the presentation 's gone!

DAISY, half aloud.

Gracious, how they glare at me!

WINTERBOURNE, hurriedly.

Take my arm. The boat 's at the wharf. (She takes his arm, and they hasten away, passing through the little gate of the parapet, where they descend and disappear. The bell of the steamer continues to ring. Mrs. Costello and her companions have watched them; as they vanish, she and Miss Durant each drop into a chair.)

MRS. COSTELLO.

They will *never* come back !

MISS DURANT, eagerly.

Is n't it your duty to go after them ?

REVERDY, between the two.

They will be lovely company for the rest of the day !

ACT SECOND.

A beautiful afternoon in the gardens of the Pincian Hill in Rome. A
view of St. Peter's in the distance.

SCENE FIRST.

WINTERBOURNE, MADAME DE KATKOFF, meeting from opposite
sides. He stands before her a moment, and kisses her hand.

WINTERBOURNE.

When, at your hotel just now, they told me you had gone
out, I was pretty sure you had come here.

MADAME. DE KATKOFF.

I always come here as soon as I arrive in Rome, for the
sake of that view. It 's an old friend of mine.

WINTERBOURNE.

Have you no old friends but that, and was n't it also — a
little — for the sake of meeting one or two of them? We
all come here, you know.

MADAME DE KATKOFF.

One or two of them? You don't mean two — you mean
one! I know you all come here, and that 's why I have
arrived early, before the crowd and the music.

WINTERBOURNE.

That 's what I was counting on. I know your tastes. I
wanted to find you alone.

MADAME DE KATKOFF.

Being alone with you is n't one of my tastes! If I had

known I should meet you, I think I should n't have left my carriage.

WINTERBOURNE.

If it 's there, at hand, you might invite me to get into it.

MADAME DE KATKOFF.

I have sent it away for half an hour, while I stretch myself a little. I have been sitting down for a week — in railway-trains.

WINTERBOURNE.

You can't escape from me, then!

MADAME DE KATKOFF.

Don't begin that way, or you 'll disappoint me. You speak as if you had received none of my letters.

WINTERBOURNE.

And you speak as if you had written me a dozen! I received three little notes.

MADAME DE KATKOFF.

They were short, but they were clear.

WINTERBOURNE.

Oh, very clear indeed! "You 're an awful nuisance, and I wish never to hear of you again." That was about the gist of them.

MADAME DE KATKOFF.

"Unless you promise not to persecute me, I won't come to Rome." That 's more how I should express it. And you did promise.

WINTERBOURNE.

I promised to try and hate you, for that seemed to be what you wished to bring me to! And I have been waiting for you these three weeks, as a man waits for his worst enemy.

MADAME DE KATKOFF.

I should be your worst enemy indeed, if I listened to you
— if I allowed you to mingle your fresh, independent life
with my own embarrassed and disillusioned one. If you
have been here three weeks, you ought to have found some
profitable occupation.

WINTERBOURNE.

You speak as if I were looking out for a job! My princi-
pal occupation has been waiting for you.

MADAME DE KATKOFF.

It must have made you pleasant company to your friends.

WINTERBOURNE.

My friends are only my aunt and the young lady who is
with her — a very good girl, but painfully prim. I have
been devoted to them, because I said to myself that after you
came —

MADAME DE KATKOFF.

You would n't have possession of your senses? So it appears. On the same principle, I hope you have shown some
attention to the little girl who was at Vevey, whom I saw you
in such a fair way to be intimate with.

WINTERBOURNE, after a silence.

What do you know about her ?

MADAME DE KATKOFF.

Nothing but that we are again at the same hotel. A
former servant of mine, a very unprincipled fellow, is now in
her mother's employ, and he was the first person I met as I
left my rooms to-day. I imagine from this that the young
lady is not far off.

WINTERBOURNE.

Not far off from *him*. I wish she were farther !

MADAME DE KATKOFF.

She struck me last summer as remarkably attractive.

WINTERBOURNE.

She 's exactly what she was last summer — only more so !

MADAME DE KATKOFF.

She must be quite enchanting, then.

WINTERBOURNE.

Do you wish me to fall in love with her ?

MADAME DE KATKOFF.

It would give me particular pleasure. I would go so far as to be the confidant of your passion.

WINTERBOURNE.

I have no passion to confide. She 's a little American flirt.

MADAME DE KATKOFF, aside.

It seems to me there is a certain passion in that !

WINTERBOURNE.

She 's foolish, frivolous, futile. She is making herself terribly talked about.

MADAME DE KATKOFF.

She looked to me very innocent — with those eyes !

WINTERBOURNE.

Oh, yes, I made a great deal of those eyes — they have the most charming lashes. But they look at too many people.

MADAME DE KATKOFF.

Should you like them to fix themselves on you ? You 're rather difficult to please. The young lady with your aunt is too grave, and this poor little person is too gay ! You had better find some one who 's between the two.

WINTERBOURNE.

You are between the two, and you won't listen to me.

MADAME DE KATKOFF.

I think I understand your country-people better than you do. I have learned a good deal about them from my observation of yourself.

WINTERBOURNE.

That must have made you very fond of them!

MADAME DE KATKOFF.

It has made me feel very kindly toward them, as you see from my interest in those young ladies. Don't judge them by what they seem. They are probably just the opposite, for that is precisely the case with yourself. Most people think you very cold, but I have discovered the truth. You are like one of those tall German stoves, which present to the eye a surface of smooth white porcelain, without the slightest symptom of fuel or of flame. Nothing at first could seem less glowing; but after you have been in the room with it for half an hour you feel that the temperature is rising — and you want to open a window!

WINTERBOURNE.

A tall German stove — that 's a very graceful comparison.

MADAME DE KATKOFF.

I am sure your grave young lady is very gay.

WINTERBOURNE.

It does n't matter; she has got a young man of her own.

MADAME DE KATKOFF.

The young man who was always with them? If you are going to be put off by a rival, I have nothing to say.

WINTERBOURNE.

He 's not a rival of mine; he 's only a rival of my aunt's. She wants me to marry Miss Durant, but Miss Durant prefers the gallant Reverdy.

6

MADAME DE KATKOFF.

That simplifies it.

WINTERBOURNE.

Not so very much; because the gallant Reverdy shows a predilection for Miss Daisy Miller.

MADAME DE KATKOFF.

Ah, then he *is* your rival!

WINTERBOURNE.

There are so many others that he does n't count. She has at least a dozen admirers, and she knocks about Rome with all of them. She once told me that she was very fond of gentlemen's society; but unfortunately they are not all gentlemen.

MADAME DE KATKOFF

So much the better chance for you.

WINTERBOURNE.

She does n't know, she can't distinguish. She is incredibly light.

MADAME DE KATKOFF.

It seems to me that you express yourself with a certain bitterness.

WINTERBOURNE.

I am not in the least in love with her, if that's what you mean. But simply as an outsider, as a spectator, as an American, I can't bear to see a nice girl — if she *is* a nice girl — expose herself to the most odious misconception. That is, if she *is* a nice girl!

MADAME DE KATKOFF.

By my little system, she ought to be very nice. If she seems very wild, depend upon it she is very tame.

WINTERBOURNE.

She has produced a fearful amount of scandal.

MADAME DE KATKOFF.

That proves she has nothing to hide. The wicked ones are not found out !

WINTERBOURNE.

She has nothing to hide but her mother, whom she conceals so effectually that no mortal eye has beheld her. Miss Daisy goes to parties alone ! When I say alone, I mean that she is usually accompanied by a foreigner with a waxed moustache and a great deal of manner. She is too nice for a foreigner !

MADAME DE KATKOFF, smiling.

As a Russian, I am greatly obliged to you !

WINTERBOURNE.

This is n't a Russian. He 's a Roman — the Cavaliere Giovanelli.

MADAME DE KATKOFF.

You spoke of a dozen, and now you have settled down to one.

WINTERBOURNE.

There were a dozen at first, but she picked them over and selected. She has made a mistake, because the man she has chosen is an adventurer.

MADAME DE KATKOFF.

An adventurer ?

WINTERBOURNE.

Oh, a very plausible one. He is very good looking, very polite ; he sings little songs at parties. He comes of a respectable family, but he has squandered his small patrimony, and he has no means of subsistence but his personal charms, which he has been hoping for the last ten years will endear him to some susceptible American heiress — whom he flatters himself he has found at last !

MADAME DE KATKOFF.

You ought to advise her — to put her on her guard.

WINTERBOURNE.

Oh, she's not serious; she is only amusing herself.

MADAME DE KATKOFF.

Try and make her serious. That's a mission for an honest man!

WINTERBOURNE, after a moment.

It's so odd to hear you defending her! It only puzzles me the more.

MADAME DE KATKOFF.

You ought to understand your countrywomen better.

WINTERBOURNE.

My countrywomen?

MADAME DE KATKOFF.

I don't mean me: I mean Miss Daisy Miller.

WINTERBOURNE.

It seems very stupid, I confess; but I have lived so long in foreign parts, among people of different manners. I mean, however, to settle the question to-day and to make up my mind. I shall meet Miss Daisy at four o'clock. I have promised to go to Mrs. Walker's.

MADAME DE KATKOFF.

And pray who is Mrs. Walker?

WINTERBOURNE.

The wife of the American consul — a very good-natured woman, who has a passion for afternoon-tea. She took up Miss Daisy when they came; she used to call her the little Flower of the West. But now she's holding the little flower in her finger-tips, at arm's length, trying to decide to let it drop.

MADAME DE KATKOFF.

Poor little flower! It must be four o'clock now.

WINTERBOURNE, looking at his watch.

You 're in a great hurry to get rid of me! Mrs. Walker's is close at hand, just beyond the Spanish Steps. I shall have time to stroll round the Pincian with you.

MADAME DE KATKOFF.

I have had strolling enough. I shall wait for my carriage.

WINTERBOURNE.

Let me at least come and see you this evening.

MADAME DE KATKOFF.

I should be delighted, but I am going to the opera.

WINTERBOURNE.

Already? The first night you are here?

MADAME DE KATKOFF.

It 's not the first; it 's the second. I am very fond of music.

WINTERBOURNE.

It 's always bad in Italy.

MADAME DE KATKOFF.

I have made provision against that in the person of the Russian ambassador, whom I have asked to come into my box.

WINTERBOURNE.

Ah, with ambassadors I stand no chance.

MADAME DE KATKOFF, smiling.

You are the greatest diplomatist of all! Good-by for the present. (She turns away. Winterbourne looks after her a moment.)

WINTERBOURNE.

You decide more easily than Mrs. Walker: you *have* dropped me!

MADAME DE KATKOFF.

Ah, but you 're not a flower! (Winterbourne looks at her an instant longer; then, with a little passionate switch of his stick, he walks off. Just as he disappears, Eugenio comes in at the back.)   And now I shall have a quiet evening with a book!

SCENE SECOND.

MADAME DE KATKOFF, EUGENIO, who enters hat in hand, with a bow.

EUGENIO.

It 's the second time to-day that I have had the pleasure of meeting Madame.

MADAME DE KATKOFF.

I should like very much to believe it would be the last!

EUGENIO, twirling his hat.

That, perhaps, is more than I can promise. We will call it the last but one; for my purpose in approaching Madame is to demand an interview — a serious interview! Seeing Madame, at a distance, in conversation with a gentleman, I waited till the gentleman had retired; for I must do Madame the justice to admit that, with Madame, the gentlemen do usually, at last, retire!

MADAME DE KATKOFF.

It 's a misfortune to me, since they leave me exposed!

EUGENIO.

Madame is not exposed; Madame is protected. So long as I have an eye on Madame, I can answer for it that she will suffer no injury.

MADAME DE KATKOFF.

You protect me as the butcher protects the lamb! I suppose you have come to name your price.

EUGENIO.

Madame goes straight to the point! I have come to name my price, but not to ask for money.

MADAME DE KATKOFF.

It's very kind of you to recognize that I have not money enough.

EUGENIO.

Madame has money enough, but the talents of Madame are still greater than her wealth. It is with the aid of these talents that I shall invite Madame to render me a service — a difficult, delicate service, but so valuable that it will release Madame from further obligations.

MADAME DE KATKOFF, ironical.

It's delightful to think of being released! I suppose the service is to recommend you as a domestic. That would be difficult, certainly.

EUGENIO.

Too difficult — for Madame! No; it is simply, as I say, to grant me an interview, when I can explain. Be so good as to name an hour when I can wait upon you.

MADAME DE KATKOFF.

In my apartments? I would rather not see you there. Explain to me here.

EUGENIO.

It's a little delicate for a public place. Besides, I have another appointment here.

MADAME DE KATKOFF.

You do a great business! If you mean that I am to wait upon *you*, we may as well drop negotiations.

EUGENIO.

Let us compromise. My appointment will end in a quarter of an hour. If at that time Madame is still on the Pincian —

MADAME DE KATKOFF.

You would like me to sit upon a bench till you are ready to attend to me?

EUGENIO.

It would have the merit of settling the matter at once, without more suspense for Madame.

MADAME DE KATKOFF, thoughtfully, aside.

That would be a merit, certainly; and I am curious about the exercise he wishes to offer my talents! (Aloud.) I shall stroll about here till my carriage comes; if you wish to take advantage of that —

EUGENIO.

To take advantage is exactly what I wish! And as this particular spot is exceptionally quiet I shall look for Madame here.

MADAME DE KATKOFF, as she strolls away.

How unspeakably odious!

EUGENIO, alone a moment, looking after her.

She shall bend till she breaks! The delay will have the merit, too, of making me sure of Giovanelli — if he only keeps the tryst! I must n't throw away a card on *her* before I 've won the game of him. But he 's such a deuced fine gentleman that there 's no playing fair! (Seeing Giovanelli, who comes in at the left.) He is up to time, though. (Bowing.) Signor Cavaliere!

SCENE THIRD.

EUGENIO, GIOVANELLI.

GIOVANELLI, very elegant, with flowers in his buttonhole; cautious, looking round him.

You might have proposed meeting in some less conspicuous spot!

EUGENIO.

In the Coliseum, at midnight ? My dear sir, we should be much more compromised if we were discovered there !

GIOVANELLI.

Oh, if you count upon our being discovered ! . . .

EUGENIO.

There is nothing so unnatural in our having a little conversation. One should never be ashamed of an accomplice!

GIOVANELLI, with a grimace, disgusted.

Don't speak of accomplices : as if we were concocting a crime !

EUGENIO.

What makes it a work of merit is my conviction that you are a perfect gentleman. If it had n't been for that, I never should have presented you to my family.

GIOVANELLI.

Your family ? You speak as if, in marrying the girl, I should become your brother-in-law.

EUGENIO.

We shall certainly be united by a very peculiar tie !

GIOVANELLI.

United — united ? I don't know about that ! After my marriage, I shall travel without a courier. (Smiling.) It will be less expensive !

EUGENIO.

In the event you speak of, I myself hardly expect to remain in the ranks. I have seen too many campaigns : I shall retire on my pension. You look as if you did not understand me.

GIOVANELLI.

Perfectly. You expect the good Mrs. Miller to make you comfortable for the rest of your days.

EUGENIO.

What I expect of the good Mrs. Miller is one thing; what I expect of you is another: and on that point we had better be perfectly clear. It was to insure perfect clearness that I proposed this little conference, which you refused to allow to take place either in your own lodgings or in some comfortable café. Oh, I know you had your reasons! You don't exhibit your little interior; and though I know a good deal about you, I don't know where you live. It does n't matter, I don't want to know: it 's enough for me that I can always find you here, amid the music and the flowers. But I can't exactly make out why you would n't meet me at a café. I would gladly have paid for a glass of beer.

GIOVANELLI.

It was just your beer I was afraid of ! I never touch the beastly stuff.

EUGENIO.

Ah, if you drink nothing but champagne, no wonder you are looking for an heiress ! But before I help you to one, let me give you a word of advice. Make the best of me, if you wish me to make the best of you. I was determined to do that when I presented you to the two most amiable women in the world.

GIOVANELLI.

I must protest against your theory that you presented me. I met Mrs. Miller at a party, as any gentleman might have done.

EUGENIO.

You met her at a party, precisely; but unless I wish it, Mrs. Miller does n't go to a party ! I let you know she was to be there, and I advised you how to proceed. For the last three weeks I have done nothing but arrange little accidents, little surprises, little occasions, of which I will do you the justice to say that you have taken excellent advantage. But the time has come when I must remind you that I have not done all this from mere admiration of your distinguished appearance. I wish your success to be *my* success!

GIOVANELLI, pleased, with a certain simplicity.

I am glad to hear you talk about my success!

EUGENIO.

Oh, there's a good deal to be said about it! Have you ever been to the circus?

GIOVANELLI.

I don't see what that has to do with it!

EUGENIO.

You've seen the bareback rider turn a somersault through the paper hoops? It's a very pretty feat, and it brings him great applause; but half the effect depends upon the poor devil — whom no one notices — who is perched upon the edge of the ring. If he did n't hold the hoop with a great deal of skill, the bareback rider would simply come down on his nose. You turn your little somersaults, Signor Cavaliere, and my young lady claps her hands; but all the while *I* 'm holding the hoop!

GIOVANELLI.

If I 'm not mistaken, that office, at the circus, is usually performed by the clown.

EUGENIO.

Take very good care, or you 'll have a fall!

GIOVANELLI.

I suppose you want to be paid for your trouble.

EUGENIO.

The point is n't that I want to be paid : that goes without saying ! But I want to be paid handsomely.

GIOVANELLI.

What do you call handsomely ?

EUGENIO.

A commission proportionate to the fortune of the young lady. I know something about that. I have in my pocket (slapping his side) the letter of credit of the Signora. She lets me carry it — for safety's sake !

GIOVANELLI.

Poor Signora ! It 's a strange game we are playing !

EUGENIO, looking at him a moment.

Oh, if you doubt of the purity of your motives, you have only to say so. You swore to me that you adored my young lady.

GIOVANELLI.

She 's an angel, and I worship the ground she treads on. That makes me wonder whether I could n't get on without you.

EUGENIO, dryly.

Try it and see. I have only to say the word, and Mrs. Miller will start to-morrow for the north.

GIOVANELLI.

And if you don't say the word, that 's another thing you want to be paid for ! It mounts up very fast.

EUGENIO.

It mounts up to fifty thousand francs, to be handed to me six months after you are married.

GIOVANELLI.

Fifty thousand francs?

EUGENIO.

The family exchequer will never miss them. Besides, I give you six months. You sign a little note, "for value received."

GIOVANELLI.

And if the marriage — if the marriage —

EUGENIO.

If the marriage comes to grief, I burn up the note.

GIOVANELLI.

How can I be sure of that?

EUGENIO.

By having already perceived that I'm not an idiot. If you don't marry, you can't pay: I need no one to tell me that. But I intend you *shall* marry.

GIOVANELLI, satirical.

It's uncommonly good of you! After all, I have n't a squint!

EUGENIO.

I picked you out for your good looks; and you're so tremendously fascinating that even when I lose patience with your want of everything else I can't afford to sacrifice you. Your prospects are now very good. The estimable mother—

GIOVANELLI.

The estimable mother believes me to be already engaged to her daughter. It shows how much she knows about it!

EUGENIO.

No, you are not engaged, but you will be, next week. You have rather too many flowers there, by the way: you overdo it a little.   (Pointing to Giovanelli's button-hole.)

GIOVANELLI.

So long as you pay for them, the more the better! How

far will it carry me to be engaged? Mr. Miller can hardly
be such a fool as his wife.

EUGENIO, *stroking his moustache.*

Mr. Miller?

GIOVANELLI.

The mysterious father, in that unpronounceable town!
He must be a man of energy, to have made such a fortune,
and the idea of his energy haunts me!

EUGENIO.

That 's because you 've got none yourself.

GIOVANELLI.

I don't pretend to that; I only pretend to — a —

EUGENIO.

To be fascinating, I know! But you 're afraid the papa
won't see it.

GIOVANELLI.

I don't exactly see why he should set his heart on a Roman son-in-law.

EUGENIO.

It 's your business to produce that miracle!

GIOVANELLI.

By making the girl talked about? My respect for her is
in proportion to the confidence she shows me. That confidence is unlimited.

EUGENIO.

Oh, unlimited! I have never seen anything like that
confidence; and if out of such a piece of cloth as that you
can't cut a coat —

GIOVANELLI.

I never pretended to be a tailor! And you must not forget that I have a rival.

EUGENIO.

Forget it? I regard it as a particularly gratifying fact. If you did n't have a rival I should have very small hopes of you.

GIOVANELLI.

I confess I don't follow you. The young lady's confidence in Mr. Winterbourne is at least equal to her confidence in me.

EUGENIO.

Ah, but *his* confidence in the young lady? That 's another affair! He thinks she goes too far. He 's an American, like herself; but there are Americans and Americans, and when they take it into their heads to open their eyes they open them very wide.

GIOVANELLI.

If you mean that this American 's a donkey, I see no reason to differ with you.

EUGENIO.

Leave him to me. I 've got a stick to beat him with!

GIOVANELLI.

You make me shiver a little! Do you mean to put him out of the way?

EUGENIO.

I mean to put him out of the way. Ah, you can trust me! I don't carry a stiletto, and if you 'll excuse me I won't describe my little plan. You 'll tell me what you think of it when you have seen the results. The great feature is simply that Miss Daisy, seeing herself abandoned —

GIOVANELLI.

Will look about her for a consoler? Ah, consolation is a specialty of mine, and if you give me a chance to console I think I shall be safe.

EUGENIO.

I shall go to work on the spot ! (Takes out his pocket-book, from which he extracts a small folded paper, holding it up a moment before Giovanelli.) Put your name to that, and send it back to me by post.

GIOVANELLI, reading the paper with a little grimace.

Fifty thousand !   Fifty thousand is steep.

EUGENIO.

Signor Cavaliere, the letter of credit is for half a million !

GIOVANELLI, pocketing the paper.

Well, give me a chance to console — give me a chance to console ! (Goes off at the back, while, at the same moment, Madame de Katkoff reappears.)

SCENE FOURTH.

EUGENIO, MADAME DE KATKOFF.

EUGENIO, perceiving her, aside.

The Katkoff — up to time ! If my second little paper works as well as my first, I have nothing to fear. (Aloud.) I am quite at the service of Madame.

MADAME DE KATKOFF.

My carriage has not come back; it was to pick up a friend at St. Peter's.

EUGENIO.

I am greatly indebted to Madame's friends. I have my little proposition ready.

MADAME DE KATKOFF.

Be so good as to let me hear it.

EUGENIO.

In three words it is this : Do me the favor to captivate Mr. Winterbourne ! Madame starts a little. She will pretend, perhaps, that Mr. Winterbourne is already captivated.

MADAME DE KATKOFF.

You have an odd idea of my pretensions! I would rather pay you a sum of money than listen to this sort of thing.

EUGENIO.

I was afraid you would be a little shocked — at first. But the proposal I make has the greatest recommendations.

MADAME DE KATKOFF.

For Mr. Winterbourne, certainly!

EUGENIO.

For Mr. Winterbourne, very plainly; but also for Madame, if she would only reflect upon the facility —

MADAME DE KATKOFF.

What do you know about facility? Your proposal is odious!

EUGENIO.

The worst is already done. Mr. Winterbourne is deeply interested in Madame.

MADAME DE KATKOFF.

His name has no place in our discussion. Be so good as not to mention it again.

EUGENIO.

It will be easy not to mention it: Madame will understand without that. She will remember, perhaps, that when I had the honor of meeting her last summer, I was in the service of a distinguished family.

MADAME DE KATKOFF.

The amiable Mrs. Miller? That name has stuck in my mind!

EUGENIO.

Permit me to regard it as a happy omen! The amiable Mrs. Miller, as I then informed Madame, has a daughter as

7

amiable as herself.   It is of the greatest importance that this young lady should be detached from the gentleman whose name I am not allowed to mention.

MADAME DE KATKOFF.

Should be detached?

EUGENIO.

If he is interested in Madame, he is also a little interested in the Signorina.   You know what men are, Madame!

MADAME DE KATKOFF.

If the Signorina is as amiable as you say, I can imagine no happier circumstance.

EUGENIO.

From the point of view of Madame, who is a little tired of the gentleman; but not from my own, who wish the young lady to make another marriage.

MADAME DE KATKOFF.

Excuse me from entering into your points of view and your marriages!

EUGENIO, abruptly.

Ah, if you choose to terminate the discussion, it wasn't worth while to wait.   (A pause.)

MADAME DE KATKOFF, aside.

It was worth while to wait — to learn what a coward I am!   (Aloud, after a moment.)   Is Miss Miller in love with Mr. Winterbourne?

EUGENIO, smiling.

I thought Madame would come to the name!   (Aside.)   It was the idea that fetched her!   (Aloud.)   Miss Miller is not, perhaps, exactly in love with Mr. Winterbourne, but she has a great appreciation of his society.   What I ask of you is to undertake that for the next two months she shall have as little of it as possible.

MADAME DE KATKOFF.

By taking as much of it myself ?   You ask me to play a very pretty part.

EUGENIO.

Madame would play it to perfection !

MADAME DE KATKOFF.

To break a young girl's heart — to act an abominable comedy ?

EUGENIO.

You won't break any one's heart, unless it be Mr. Winterbourne's — which will serve him right for being so tiresome. As for the comedy, remember that the best actresses receive the highest salary.

MADAME DE KATKOFF.

If I had been a good actress, you never would have got me into your power.   What do you propose to do with your little American ?

EUGENIO.

To marry her to a Roman gentleman.   All I ask of you is to use a power you already have.   I know that of late it has suited your pleasure not to use it : you have tried to keep Mr. Winterbourne at a distance.   But call him a little nearer, and you will see that he will come !

MADAME DE KATKOFF.

So that the girl may see it too ?   Your ingenuity does you great honor.   I don't believe in your Roman gentleman.

EUGENIO.

It is not necessary that you should believe.   Believe only that on the day the Signorina becomes engaged to the irreproachable person I have selected, I will place in your hands the document which I hold at your disposition.

MADAME DE KATKOFF.

How am I to be sure of that?

EUGENIO, aside.

They all want to be sure! (Aloud.) Nothing venture, nothing have!

MADAME DE KATKOFF.

And if she never becomes engaged?

EUGENIO.

Ah, then, I confess, I must still hold the document. (Aside.) That will make her work for it! (Aloud.) Why should you trouble yourself with irrelevant questions? Your task is perfectly definite. Occupy Mr. Winterbourne, and leave the rest to me.

MADAME DE KATKOFF.

I must tell you — disagreeable as it may be to me to do so — that I shall have to make a very sudden turn.

EUGENIO.

It will be all the more effective. (Complacently.) Sudden turns are the essence of fascination!

MADAME DE KATKOFF, aside.

It's insufferable to discuss with him! But if there's a hope — if there's a hope . . . (Aloud.) I told Mr. Winterbourne, not an hour ago, that I wished never to see him again.

EUGENIO.

I can imagine no more agreeable surprise to him, then, than to be told, half an hour hence, that you can't live without him! You know the things the ladies say! Don't be afraid of being sudden: he'll think it the more romantic. For you those things are easy, Madame (bowing low); for you those things are easy. I leave the matter to your consideration. (Aside, as he goes off.) She'll do it! (Exit.)

MADAME DE KATKOFF, alone a moment.

Those things are easy — those things are easy? They
are easier, perhaps, than paying out half one's fortune.
(Stands a moment thoughtful, then gives a little nervous gesture, as of decision.)
If I give him leave to come to the opera, I must go myself
— to Italian music! But an hour or two of Donizetti, for
the sake of one's comfort! . . . He said he would come
back — from the wife of the consul. (Looking about her, she goes
out.)

SCENE FIFTH.

DAISY, then GIOVANELLI.

DAISY, coming in with a certain haste, and glancing behind her.

It 's a pity you can't walk in Rome without every one
staring so! And now he 's not here — he 's not where he
said he would be. I don't care. He 's very nice, but I
certainly shan't go and look for him. I 'll just wait a little.
Perhaps, if I don't walk round, they won't stare at me so
much. I did n't say good-by to Mrs. Walker, because she
was talking to Mr. Winterbourne, and I shan't go near
Mr. Winterbourne again till he comes near me. Half an
hour in the room, and never within ten yards of me! He
looks so pleasant when he talks — even when he talks to
other girls. He 's always talking to other girls, and not
even to girls — to old women, and gentlemen, and foreigners.
I 've done something he does n't like, I 'm very sure of that.
He does n't like anything — anything that *I* do. It 's hard
to know what he *does* like! He 's got such peculiar tastes
— from his foreign education; you can't ever tell where
you 'll find him. Well, I have n't had a foreign education,
and I don't see that I 'm any the worse for that. If I 'd had

a foreign education, I might as well give up ! I should n't be able to breathe, for fear I was breathing wrong. There seem to be so many ways, over here ! But I only know one way, and I don't see why I should learn the others when there are people who do like — who do like — what I do. They say they do, at any rate, and they say it so prettily ! The English say it very nicely, but the Italians say it best. As for the Americans, they don't say it at all, and Mr. Winterbourne less than any of them ! Well, I don't care so much about the Americans : I can make it all right with the Americans when I get home. Mr. Winterbourne is n't an American ; I never saw any one like *him* over there. If I had, perhaps I should n't have come away ; for over there it would all be different. Well, it is n't different here, and I suppose it never will be. Everything is strange over here ; and what is strangest of all is one's liking people that are so peculiar. (Stands thoughtful a moment, then rouses herself.) There 's Mr. Giovanelli — a mile off. Does he suppose I wish to communicate with him by signs ? (Giovanelli comes in, hat in hand, with much eagerness.)

GIOVANELLI.

I have looked for you everywhere !

DAISY.

Well, I was n't everywhere ; I was here.

GIOVANELLI.

Standing all alone, without a protector !

DAISY.

I was n't more alone than I was at Mrs. Walker's.

GIOVANELLI, smiling, slightly fatuous.

Because *I* was not there ?

DAISY.

Oh, it was n't the people who were *not* there ! (Aside.) If

they had known I was coming, I suppose there would n't
have been any one !

GIOVANELLI, in an attitude of the most respectful admiration.

How can I sufficiently thank you for granting me this
supreme satisfaction ?

DAISY.

That's a very fine name to give to a walk on the Pincian.
You had better put on your hat.

GIOVANELLI.

You wish to escape notice ? Perhaps you are right.
That was why I did n't come to Mrs. Walker's, whose parties
are so charming ! I thought that if we slipped away together it might attract attention.

DAISY.

Do you mean they would have thought it improper ? They
would have thought it still more improper to see me leaving
alone ; so I did n't say a word to any one — only mother.

GIOVANELLI.

Ah, you told your admirable parent ? She is with us,
then, in spirit !

DAISY.

She wanted to get away herself, if that's what you mean ;
but she did n't feel as if she could leave till Eugenio came
for her.   And Eugenio seems to have so much to do to-day.

GIOVANELLI.

It is doubtless in your interest.   He is a very faithful
servant.

DAISY.

Well, he told mother she must stay there an hour : he had
some business of importance.

GIOVANELLI.

Let us hope that his business is done, and that the patient
Mrs. Miller is released.

DAISY.

She was patient enough when I told her I should n't come to dinner.

GIOVANELLI, starting, with an air of renewed devotion.

Am I to understand that you have consented to my little fantasy?

DAISY.

Of dining at that old tavern, where the artists go?

GIOVANELLI.

The renowned and delightful *Falcone*, in the heart of ancient Rome! You are a person of delicious surprises! The other day, you would n't listen to it.

DAISY.

I don't remember the other day: all I know is, I 'll go now. (Aside.) The other day Mr. Winterbourne spoke to me!

GIOVANELLI.

My dear young lady, you make me very happy!

DAISY.

By going to eat macaroni with you?

GIOVANELLI.

It is n't the macaroni; it 's the sentiment!

DAISY.

The sentiment is yours, not mine. I have n't any: it 's all gone!

GIOVANELLI.

Well, I shan't complain if I find myself at table with you in a dusky corner of that picturesque little cook-shop, where the ceiling is black, and the walls are brown, and the floor is red!

DAISY, watching him as he describes it.

Oh dear! it must be very lovely.

GIOVANELLI.

And the old wine-flasks, covered with plaited straw, are as big round — are much bigger round — than your waist!

DAISY.

That's just what I want to see. Let's go there at once!

GIOVANELLI, consulting his watch.

Half-past four. Is n't that rather soon to dine?

DAISY.

We can go on foot through the old streets. I'm dying to see them on foot.

GIOVANELLI, aside.

That will be cheaper than a cab! (Aloud.) We should get there at five — a little early still. Might n't we first take a few turns round this place?

DAISY, after a pause.

Oh, yes, if you like.

GIOVANELLI, aside.

I should like my creditors to see! (Aloud.) Perhaps it does n't suit you: you are a little afraid.

DAISY.

What should I be afraid of?

GIOVANELLI, smiling.

Not of meeting your mother, I know!

DAISY.

If I had been afraid, I should n't have come.

GIOVANELLI.

That is perfect. But let me say one thing: you have a way of taking the meaning from the favors you bestow.

DAISY.

The meaning? They have n't got any meaning!

GIOVANELLI, vaguely.

Ah!   (Mrs. Costelle, Miss Durant, and Charles Reverdy appear.)

DAISY, looking at Mrs. Costello and Miss Durant.

Unless it be to make those dreadful women glower! How d' ye do, Mr. Reverdy?

GIOVANELLI, smiling.

I see you are not afraid!   (He goes out with her.)

SCENE SIXTH.

MRS. COSTELLO, MISS DURANT, CHARLES REVERDY.

MISS DURANT.

She has grown to look very hard.

MRS. COSTELLO.

The gentleman looks soft, and that makes up for it.

MISS DURANT.

Do you call him a gentleman?

MRS. COSTELLO.

Ah, compared with the courier! She has a different one every time.

REVERDY, with the camp-stool, aside.

A different one every time, but never, alas, *this* one!

MRS. COSTELLO.

There 's one comfort in it all: she has given up Frederick.

MISS DURANT.

Ah, she goes too far even for him!

REVERDY.

Too far with other men: that 's the trouble! With him she went as far as the Castle of Chillon.

MRS. COSTELLO.

Don't recall that episode. Heaven only knows what happened there.

REVERDY.

I know what happened : he was awfully sold. That's why he let you carry him off.

MRS. COSTELLO.

Much good it did us ! I'm very much disappointed in Frederick.

MISS DURANT.

I can't imagine what you expected of him.

MRS. COSTELLO.

I expected him to fall in love with you — or to marry you, at any rate.

MISS DURANT.

You would have been still more disappointed, then, if I had refused him.

MRS. COSTELLO, dryly.

I should have been surprised.

REVERDY, sentimentally.

Would you have refused him, Miss Durant ?

MISS DURANT.

Yes, on purpose to spite you. You don't understand ? It takes a man to be stupid ! If Mr. Winterbourne were to marry some one else, it would leave Miss Daisy Miller free.

REVERDY.

Free to walk about with the native population ? She seems to be free enough already. Mrs. Costello, the camp-stool is at your service.

MRS. COSTELLO.

Give it to me, and I will go and sit in the shade. Excuse

me, I would rather carry it myself. (Taking the camp-stool, aside to Miss Durant.) If he proposes, mind you accept him.

MISS DURANT.

If who proposes ?

MRS. COSTELLO.

Our young companion ! He is manœuvring to get rid of me. He has nothing but his expectations, but his expectations are of the best. (She marches away with her camp-stool, and seats herself at a distance, where, with her eyeglass raised, she appears to look at what goes on in another part of the garden.)

MISS DURANT, aside.

Am *I* one of his expectations ? Fortunately, I don't need to marry for money. (Aloud.) Cousin Louisa is furious with me for not being more encouraging to Mr. Winterbourne. I don't know what she would have liked me to do !

REVERDY.

You have been very proper, very dignified.

MISS DURANT.

That's the way I was brought up. I never liked him, from the first.

REVERDY.

Oh, he's a stupid stick !

MISS DURANT.

I don't say he's stupid — and he's very good looking.

REVERDY.

As good looking as a man can be in whom one feature — the most expressive — has been entirely omitted. He has got no eyes in his head.

MISS DURANT.

No eyes ?

REVERDY.

To see that that poor little creature is in love with him.

MISS DURANT.

She has a queer way of showing it.

REVERDY.

Ah, they always have queer ways!

MISS DURANT.

He sees it, but he does n't care.

REVERDY.

That 's still worse, — the omission not of a feature, but of an organ (tapping his heart and smiling), the seat of our purest and highest joys!

MISS DURANT, aside.

Cousin Louisa was right! (Aloud.) Do you mean that he has no heart?

REVERDY.

If he had as big a one as the rosette on your shoe, would he leave me here to do all the work?

MISS DURANT, looking at her foot.

The rosette on my shoe is rather big.

REVERDY, looking as well.

It is n't so much the size of the rosette as the smallness of the shoe!

MISS DURANT, aside.

Cousin Louisa is certainly right! (Aloud, smiling.) Yours, I suppose, is bigger than that.

REVERDY.

My shoe? I should think so — rather!

MISS DURANT.

Dear, no! I mean your heart. Though I don't think it 's at all nice in you to complain of being left with us.

REVERDY.

When I am left with you, I don't complain; but when I am left with *her!* (Indicating Mrs. Costello.)

MISS DURANT.

Well, you are not with her now.

REVERDY.

Ah, now it's very pleasant.   Only she has got the camp-stool.

MISS DURANT.

Do you want it for yourself ?

REVERDY.

Yes; I have been carrying it for the last six months, and I feel rather awkward without it.   It gives one confidence to have something in one's hand.

MISS DURANT.

Good heavens !   What do you want to do ?

REVERDY.

I want to make you a little speech.

MISS DURANT.

You will do very well as you are.

REVERDY.

I'll try it.   (In an attitude.)   Six months ago I had moments of rebellion, but to-day I have come to love my chains ! Accordingly — (Mrs. Costello starts up and hurries forward, the camp-stool in her hand.)   By Jove ! if she hears me, she'll rivet them faster.

MRS. COSTELLO, seizing Miss Durant's arm.

My poor, dear child, whom do you think I've seen ?

REVERDY.

By your expression, the ghost of Julius Cæsar !

MRS. COSTELLO.

The Russian woman — the princess — whom we saw last summer.

MISS DURANT.

Well, my dear cousin, she won't eat us up !

MRS. COSTELLO.

No, but she 'll eat Frederick !

REVERDY.

On the contrary, her appetite for Frederick is small.   Don't
you remember that, last summer, she left the hotel as soon
as he arrived ?

MRS. COSTELLO.

That was only a feint, to put us off the scent.   He has
been in secret correspondence with her, and their meeting
here is prearranged.

MISS DURANT.

I don't know why you call their correspondence secret,
when he was always going to the post-office !

MRS. COSTELLO.

Ah, but you can't tell what he did there !   Frederick is
very deep.

REVERDY.

There 's nothing secret, at any rate, about her arrival here.
She alighted yesterday at our own hotel, in the most public
manner, with the landlord and all the waiters drawn up to
receive her.   It did n't occur to me to mention it.

MRS. COSTELLO.

I don't really know what you are with us for !

MISS DURANT.

Oh, Cousin Louisa, he is meant for better things than
that !

MRS. COSTELLO, to Miss Durant, aside.

Do you mean that he has proposed ?

MISS DURANT.

No, but he was just going to.

MRS. COSTELLO, disappointed.

Ah, you have told me that before !

MISS DURANT.

Because you never give him time.

MRS. COSTELLO.

Does he want three hours?

MISS DURANT.

No, but he wants three minutes!

REVERDY, who has strolled away, observing them, aside.

Happy thought, to make them fight about me! Mutual destruction would ensue, and I should be master of the situation. (Aloud.) I am only a man, dear Madam; I am not a newspaper.

MRS. COSTELLO.

If you only were, we could stop our subscription! And, as a proof of what I say, here comes Frederick, to look after his Russian. (Winterbourne comes in, with Mrs. Walker.)

REVERDY.

With the wife of the consul, to look after him!

———

SCENE SEVENTH.

MRS. COSTELLO, MISS DURANT, REVERDY, WINTERBOURNE, MRS. WALKER.

MRS. WALKER.

Oh, you dreadful people, what are you doing here, when you ought to be at my reception?

MRS. COSTELLO.

We were just thinking of going; it's so very near.

MRS. WALKER.

Only round the corner! But there are better reasons than that.

MISS DURANT.

There can hardly be a very good one, when you yourself have come away!

MRS. WALKER.

You would never imagine what has brought me!   I have come in pursuit of little Daisy Miller.

MRS. COSTELLO.

And you have brought my nephew to help you!

WINTERBOURNE.

A walk in such charming company is a privilege not to be lost.   Perhaps, dear aunt, you can give us news.

MRS. COSTELLO.

Of that audacious and desperate person?   Dear me, yes. We met her just now, on the arm of a dreadful man.

MRS. WALKER.

Oh, we are too late then.   She is lost!

MRS. COSTELLO.

It seems to me she was lost long ago, and (significantly, at Winterbourne) that this is not the first rendezvous she has taken.

WINTERBOURNE, smiling.

If it does her no more harm than the others, Mrs. Walker had better go back to her teapot!

REVERDY, to Miss Durant.

That's an allusion to the way he was sold!

MRS. WALKER.

She left my house, half an hour ago, without a word to any one but her idiot of a mother, who thought it all right that she should walk off to the Pincian to meet the hand-some Giovanelli.   I only discovered her flight just now, by a lady who was coming in at the moment that Miss Daisy,

8

shaking out her little flounces and tossing up her little head, tripped away from my door, to fall into the arms of a cavalier !

MISS DURANT.

Into his arms ?　Ah, Mrs. Walker !

MRS. WALKER.

My dear young lady, with these unscrupulous foreigners one can never be sure.　You know as well as I what becomes of the reputation of a girl who shows herself in this place, at this hour, with all the rank and fashion of Rome about her, with no more responsible escort than a gentleman renowned for his successes !

REVERDY, to Miss Durant.

It 's as if you were here with me, you know !

MRS. WALKER.

This idea came over me with a kind of horror, and I determined to save her if I could.

MRS. COSTELLO.

There is nothing left of her to save !

MRS. WALKER.

There is always something left, and my representative position makes it a duty.　My rooms were filled with guests — a hundred and fifty people — but I put on my bonnet and seized Mr. Winterbourne's arm.

WINTERBOURNE.

You can testify that I did n't wince !　I quite agree with you as to the importance of looking her up.　Foreigners never understand.

REVERDY, aside.

My dear fellow, if they understand no better than you ! . . .

MRS. WALKER.

What I want of you dear people is to go and entertain

my visitors. Console them for my absence, and tell them I shall be back in five minutes.

MISS DURANT.

It will be very nice to give a reception without any trouble.

MRS. COSTELLO.

Without any trouble — scarcely! But there is nothing we would n't do —

MRS. WALKER.

For the representative of one's country! Be charming, then, as you can so well. (Seeing Daisy and Giovanelli come in.) I shall not be long, for by the mercy of Heaven the child is guided to this spot!

REVERDY.

If you think you have only to pick her up, we won't wait for you! (He goes out with Mrs. Costello and Miss Durant.)

SCENE EIGHTH.

MRS. WALKER, WINTERBOURNE, DAISY, GIOVANELLI.

WINTERBOURNE, as the two others slowly come in together, not at first seeing him.

We shall have a siege: she won't give him up for the asking.

MRS. WALKER.

We must divide our forces, then. You will deal with Daisy.

WINTERBOURNE.

I would rather attack the gentleman.

MRS. WALKER.

No, no; there 'll be trouble. Mr. Giovanelli, I should like a little conversation with you.

GIOVANELLI, starting, and coming forward; very polite.

You do me great honor, Madame!

MRS. WALKER.

I wish to scold you for not coming to me to-day ; but to spare your blushes, it must be in private.   (Strolls away with him, out of sight.)

DAISY, aside.

They have come to take me away.   Ah, they are very cruel !

WINTERBOURNE.

I had no chance to speak to you at Mrs. Walker's, and I have come to make up for my loss.

DAISY, looking at him a moment.

What is Mrs. Walker doing here !   Why does n't she stay with her guests ?

WINTERBOURNE.

I brought her away — to do just what she has done.

DAISY.

To take away Mr. Giovanelli ?   I don't understand you.

WINTERBOURNE.

A great many people think that you understand, but that you don't care.

DAISY.

I don't care what people think.   I have done no harm.

WINTERBOURNE.

That 's exactly what I say — you don't care.   But I wish you would care a little, for your friends are very much frightened.   When Mrs. Walker ascertained that you had left her house alone, and had come to meet a gentleman here — here, where all Rome assembles at this hour to amuse itself, and where you would be watched and criticised and calumniated — when Mrs. Walker made this discovery, she said but three words — "To the rescue ! "   But she took her plunge, as if you had been drowning.

DAISY.

And you jumped overboard, too !

WINTERBOURNE.

Oh dear, no ; I 'm standing on the brink. I only interpret her sentiments. I don't express my own.

DAISY.

They would interest me more than Mrs. Walker's ; but I don't see what either of you have to do with me.

WINTERBOURNE.

We admire you very much, and we hate to see you misjudged.

DAISY.

I don't know what you mean, and I don't know what you think I want to do.

WINTERBOURNE.

I have n't the least idea about that. All I mean is that if you could see, as I see it, how little it 's the custom here to do what you do, and how badly it looks to fly in the face of the custom, you would be a little more on your guard.

DAISY.

I know nothing about the custom. I 'm an American ; I 'm not one of these people.

WINTERBOURNE.

In that case, you would behave differently. Your being an American is just the point. You are a very conspicuous American, thanks to your attractions, to your charms, to the publicity of your life. Such people, with the best intentions in the world, are often very indiscreet ; and it 's to save the reputation of her compatriots that the fairest and brightest of American girls should sacrifice a little of her independence.

DAISY.

Look here, Mr. Winterbourne, you make too much fuss:
that 's what 's the matter with you!

WINTERBOURNE.

If I make enough to persuade you to go home with Mrs.
Walker, my highest ambition will be gratified.

DAISY.

I think you are trying to mystify me: I can tell that by
your language. One would never think you were the same
person who went with me to that castle.

WINTERBOURNE.

I am not quite the same, but I have a good deal in common with him. Now, Mr. Giovanelli does n't resemble that
person at all.

DAISY, coldly.

I don't know why you speak to me about Mr. Giovanelli.

WINTERBOURNE.

Because — because Mrs. Walker asked me to.

DAISY.

It would be better if she should do it herself.

WINTERBOURNE.

That 's exactly what I told her; but she had an odd fancy
that I have a kind of influence with you.

DAISY, with expression.

Poor Mrs. Walker!

WINTERBOURNE.

Poor Mrs. Walker! She does n't know that no one has
any influence with you — that you do nothing in the world
but what pleases yourself.

DAISY.

Whom, then, am I to please? The people that think
such dreadful things of me? I don't even understand what

they think! What do you mean, about my reputation? I have n't got any reputation! If people are so cruel and wicked, I am sure I would rather not know it. In America they let me alone, and no one ran after me, like Mrs. Walker. It 's natural I should like the people who seem to like me, and who will take the trouble to go round with me. The others may say what they like. I can't understand Italian, and I should never hear of it if you did n't come and translate.

WINTERBOURNE.

It 's not only the Italians — it 's the Americans.

DAISY.

Do you mean your aunt and your cousin? I don't know why I should make myself miserable for *them!*

WINTERBOURNE.

I mean every one who has ever had the very questionable advantage of making your acquaintance — only to be subjected to the torment of being unable either to believe in you or to doubt of you.

DAISY.

To doubt of me? You are very strange!

WINTERBOURNE.

You are stranger still. But I did n't come here to reason with you: that would be vain, for we speak a different language, and we should n't understand each other. I only came to say to you, in the most respectful manner, that if you should consult your best interests you would go home with Mrs. Walker.

DAISY.

Do you think I had such a lovely time there, half an hour ago, when you did n't so much as look at me?

WINTERBOURNE.

If I had spoken to you, would you have stayed?

DAISY.

After I had an engagement here? (With a little laugh.) I must say, you expect a great deal!

WINTERBOURNE, looking at her a moment.

What they say is true — you are a thorough-going coquette!

(Mrs. Walker reappears, with Giovanelli.)

DAISY.

You speak too much of what they say. To escape from you, I'll go anywhere!

MRS. WALKER, to Winterbourne, while Giovanelli speaks to Daisy.

He's very accommodating, when you tell him that if Mrs. Miller gets frightened she will start off for America.

WINTERBOURNE.

It's more than I can say of Miss Daisy!

MRS. WALKER.

Have you had no success?

WINTERBOURNE.

I have had my ears boxed!

MRS. WALKER, to Daisy.

My precious child, you escaped from my drawing-room before I had half the talk we wanted.

DAISY.

Are they all waiting there to see me brought back?

MRS. WALKER.

Oh dear, no; they have plenty to think about — with Mrs. Costello and Miss Durant.

DAISY.

Ah, those ladies are there? Then I certainly shan't go back.

MRS. WALKER, alarmed.

Hush! They 're relations of Mr. Winterbourne.

DAISY.

All the more reason for my hating them!

MRS. WALKER, to Winterbourne.

You must excuse her; she is very wicked to-day! (To Daisy.) If you won't go home, then I 'll stay with you here. Mr. Giovanelli, you promised me you would go to my house.

GIOVANELLI.

I am at the orders of Mademoiselle.

DAISY.

You may do what you please till dinner-time.

WINTERBOURNE, aside.

Gracious heavens! is she going to dine with him? (Aloud, to Daisy.) We were interrupted, but I have a great deal more to say.

DAISY.

More of the same sort? It will be a pleasure to hear that!

WINTERBOURNE.

What 's coming is a great deal better. — Do you dine at your table d'hóte?

DAISY.

Oh, yes. Randolph likes the table d'hôte.

WINTERBOURNE.

I will ask for a place there this evening, and, with your permission, it shall be next to yours.

DAISY.

I am very sorry, but I am not sure of this evening.

WINTERBOURNE, *gravely.*

That 's a great disappointment to me. (A short silence.)

MRS. WALKER, *to Giovanelli.*

You promised me you would go to my house!

GIOVANELLI.

As a man of honor, then, I must go. But I assure you, Mademoiselle (to Daisy,) that I soon return.

DAISY.

As soon as you like! (Giovanelli walks away. To Winterbourne.) Can't you come some other night?

WINTERBOURNE.

Oh, yes, by waiting a little. But with the uncertainty of your stay in Rome, this would be always something gained.

DAISY.

What will you do after dinner?

WINTERBOURNE.

• With your kind permission, I will adjourn with you to your mother's sitting-room.

DAISY.

You are very devoted, all of a sudden!

WINTERBOURNE.

Better late than never!

DAISY.

You are just as you were at that castle!

WINTERBOURNE.

So are you — at this moment. We can dream we are in that happy place!

DAISY, *aside.*

He can do with me what he will. (Aloud, quickly.) I'll tell them to keep you a seat!

WINTERBOURNE.

I shall be indebted to you forever!

DAISY.

Oh, if I don't see about it, they'll put you at the other end.

WINTERBOURNE.

Next you — that's the point.

DAISY.

Between me and Randolph !   At half past six !

WINTERBOURNE.

At half past six.

MRS. WALKER, to Winterbourne.

You can go about your business.   I have something to say to her alone.

DAISY.

Don't forget half past six !

WINTERBOURNE.

Never in the world.   At half past six !   (Walks away.)

MRS. WALKER, alone with Daisy.

And now may I be permitted to inquire whether you had arranged to dine with that Italian ?

DAISY, smiling.

In the heart of ancient Rome !   But don't tell Mr. Winterbourne what I gave up !

MRS. WALKER, aside.

I'll get you out of Rome to-morrow !   (Aloud.)   I must show you to the crowd — with *me*.   (Goes out leading Daisy.)

SCENE NINTH.

REVERDY, RANDOLPH.

REVERDY, coming in just as the others pass out, and completing Mrs. Walker's phrase.

The wife of the American consul !   The American consul is all very well, but I'll be hanged if I'll carry on the business! It's quite enough to do odd jobs for Mrs. Costello, without taking service at the consulate. Fifty carriages before the door, and five hundred people up-stairs. My companions may get up if they can! It's the first time to-day I've had a moment for a quiet smoke. (Lights a cigar, and while he is doing so Randolph comes in.) O Lord, the Old Man of the Sea!

RANDOLPH, planted before Reverdy.

I say, Mr. Reverdy, suppose you offer me a cigar.

REVERDY.

My poor child, my cigars are as big as yourself!

RANDOLPH.

There's nothing fit to smoke over here. You can't get 'em as you can in America.

REVERDY.

Yes, they're better in America (smoking); but they cost a good deal more.

RANDOLPH.

I don't care what I pay. I've got all the money I want.

REVERDY.

Don't spend it; keep it till you grow up.

RANDOLPH.

Oh, I ain't going to grow up. I've been this way for ever so long. Mother brought me over to see if I would n't start, but I have n't started an inch. You can't start in this old country.

REVERDY.

The Romans were rather tall.

RANDOLPH.

I don't care for the Romans. A child's as good as a man.

REVERDY.

The future of democracy! You remind me of the infant Hannibal.

RANDOLPH.

There's one good thing : so long as I'm little, my mother can't see me.   She's looking all round.

REVERDY.

I was going to ask you if she allowed you to mingle in this human maze.

RANDOLPH.

Mother's in the carriage, but I jumped out.

REVERDY.

Imprudent little man!   At the risk of breaking your neck?

RANDOLPH.

Oh, we were crawling along — we haven't American trotters. I saw you walking about, and when mother wasn't looking I just dropped. As soon as she missed me, she began to howl!

REVERDY.

I am sorry to be the occasion of a family broil.

RANDOLPH.

She thinks I am run over; she has begun to collect a crowd.

REVERDY.

You wicked little person!   I must take you straight back to her.

RANDOLPH.

I thought you might like to know where my sister is.

REVERDY.

At the present moment my anxiety is about your mother.

RANDOLPH.

Daisy's gone on a bender.   If you 'll give me a cigar, I 'll put you up to it.

REVERDY.

You 're a vulgar little boy.   Take me instantly to your mother.

RANDOLPH, very sarcastic.

Would n't you like to carry me on your back?

REVERDY.

If you don't come, I 'll take you under my arm. (Starts to seize him.)

RANDOLPH, dodging.

I won't come, then!

REVERDY.

Damn the little wretch! I *must* relieve his mother. (Makes another attempt to capture Randolph, who escapes, while Reverdy gives chase, and they disappear.)

SCENE TENTH.

WINTERBOURNE, then MADAME DE KATKOFF.

WINTERBOURNE, coming in alone.

Remarkable family, the Millers! Mrs. Miller, standing up in her carriage, in the centre of a crowd of Italians, and chattering to them in her native tongue. She falls upon my neck when she sees me, and announces that the gifted Randolph is no more. He has tumbled out of the vehicle, and been trampled to death! We institute a search for his remains, and as it proves fruitless she begs me to come and look for him here. (Looking round him.) I don't perceive any remains! He has mingled in the giddy throng, and the giddy throng may bring him back! It 's the business of that ruffian of a courier! (Seeing Madame de Katkoff, aside.) Is *she* still here? (Aloud.) To meet you again is better fortune than I hoped.

MADAME DE KATKOFF, strolling in slowly, with an air of deliberation, and standing a moment thoughtful.

Will you do me the favor to dine with me to-night?

WINTERBOURNE, startled.

To dine with you to-night?

MADAME DE KATKOFF.

You stare as if I were a ghost! It's very simple: to dine with me to-night, at seven o'clock, at the Hôtel de Paris?

WINTERBOURNE, aside.

It's a little awkward. (Aloud.) Do you dine at the table d'hôte?

MADAME DE KATKOFF.

At the table d'hôte, with that rabble of tourists? I dine in my own apartments.

WINTERBOURNE.

I supposed you had left the Pincian; I had no idea you were lingering.

MADAME DE KATKOFF.

Apparently I had a purpose, which you seem quite unable to appreciate. You are very slow in accepting!

WINTERBOURNE.

To tell you the honest truth, I have made an engagement.

MADAME DE KATKOFF.

An engagement? A moment ago you were dying to spend the evening with me.

WINTERBOURNE.

A moment ago you would n't listen to me.

MADAME DE KATKOFF, after a pause.

My dear friend, you are very stupid, A woman does n't confess the truth at the first summons!

WINTERBOURNE.

You are very strange. I accepted an invitation just after we parted.

MADAME DE KATKOFF.

Send word you can't come.

WINTERBOURNE.

It was from the young lady you recommended me so strongly to turn my attention to.

MADAME DE KATKOFF.

Ah, she gives invitations ?

WINTERBOURNE.

I confess I asked for this one. They are also at the Hôtel de Paris, and they dine at the table d'hôte.

MADAME DE KATKOFF.

A charming place to carry on a courtship !

WINTERBOURNE.

It 's not a courtship — however much I may have wished to please you.

MADAME DE KATKOFF.

Your wish to please me has suddenly diminished. Apparently, I am to understand that you refuse !

WINTERBOURNE.

Even when you are kind, there 's something cruel in it ! — I will dine with you with pleasure.

MADAME DE KATKOFF.

Send word, then, to your little American.

WINTERBOURNE.

Yes, I will send word. (Aside.) That 's uncommonly rough ! (Aloud.) After dinner, I suppose, you will go to the opera.

MADAME DE KATKOFF.

I don't know about the opera. (Looking at him a moment.) It will be a splendid night. How should you like a moonlight drive ?

WINTERBOURNE.

A moonlight drive — with you ? It seems to me you mock me !

MADAME DE KATKOFF, in the same tone.

To wander through the old streets, when everything is still; to see the solemn monuments wrapped up in their shadows; to watch the great fountains turn to silver in the moonshine — that has always been a dream of mine! We will try it to-night.

WINTERBOURNE, affected by her tone.

We will see the great square of St. Peter's; we will dip our hands in the Fountain of Trevi! You must be strangely beautiful in the moonlight.

MADAME DE KATKOFF.

I don't know. You shall see.

WINTERBOURNE.

What will you do with the Russian ambassador?

MADAME DE KATKOFF.

Send him about his business.

WINTERBOURNE.

An ambassador! For me?

MADAME DE KATKOFF.

Don't force me to say it; I shall make you too vain.

WINTERBOURNE.

I am not used to being treated so, and I can't help feeling that it may be only a refinement of cruelty.

MADAME DE KATKOFF.

If I have been cruel before, it was in self-defence. I have been sorely troubled, and I don't pretend to be consistent. Women are never so — especially women who love!

WINTERBOURNE.

I ask no questions; I only thank you.

MADAME DE KATKOFF.

At seven o'clock, then.

WINTERBOURNE.

You are very strange; but you are only the more ador-able.   At seven o'clock !

MADAME DE KATKOFF.

You are not to come with me; my carriage is there. (Aside, as she leaves him.)   Ingenuous young man !

WINTERBOURNE, alone, standing a moment in thought.

"Women are never consistent — especially women who love ! "   I have waited three years, but it was worth waiting for !   (Mrs. Walker comes in with Daisy, without his seeing them·)

SCENE ELEVENTH.

WINTERBOURNE, MRS. WALKER, DAISY, then EUGENIO and GIOVANELLI.

DAISY.

Well, Mr. Winterbourne, is that the way you look for my brother ?   You had better not come to dinner unless you find him.

WINTERBOURNE.

I was just wondering which way I had better go.

MRS. WALKER.

Mrs. Miller has pressed us into the service, and she wants every one to go in a different direction.   But I prefer (significantly) that Daisy and I should stick together.

DAISY, happily.

Oh, I don't care now.   You may take me anywhere !

WINTERBOURNE, aside.

Poor little thing !   And I have got to disappoint her! (Aloud.)   I suppose I had better separate from you, then.

EUGENIO, arriving hastily.

Mr. Randolph has been found — by Mr. Reverdy! (To Daisy.) If I leave your mother a moment, a misfortune is sure to arrive.

MRS. WALKER, aside.

The misfortune, indeed, is his being found! (To Daisy.) If you will join your mother, I will go back to my guests (seeing Giovanelli) — whom Mr. Giovanelli has already deserted.

GIOVANELLI, coming in.

Your guests have deserted me, Madame. They have left your house in a caravan, unable to support your absence.

MRS. WALKER, to Daisy.

I have offended all my friends for you, my dear. You ought to be grateful.

DAISY.

The reason they left was not because you came away, but because you did n't bring me back. They wanted to glare at me.

GIOVANELLI, with a little laugh.

They glared at me a good deal!

MRS. WALKER.

I will admit that they don't like you. (To Daisy.) Let me place you in your mother's hands.

EUGENIO, with importance.

I will take charge of my young lady, Madame.

WINTERBOURNE, to Daisy.

Before you go, just let me say a word.

DAISY.

As many as you please — only you frighten me!

WINTERBOURNE.

I am rather frightened myself. I am very much afraid I shall not be able to dine to-night.

DAISY.

Not be able — after your promise?

WINTERBOURNE.

It's very true I promised, and I am greatly ashamed. But a most unexpected obstacle has sprung up. I am obliged to take back my word — I am exceedingly sorry.

MRS. WALKER, in a low voice to Winterbourne.

Ah, my dear sir, you're making a mess!

DAISY.

Your obstacle must have come very quickly.

WINTERBOURNE.

Only five minutes ago.

EUGENIO, aside.

The Katkoff's as good as her word!

DAISY, much agitated.

Well, Mr. Winterbourne, I can only say I too am very sorry.

WINTERBOURNE.

I will come the very first evening I am free.

DAISY.

I didn't want the first evening; I wanted this one.

WINTERBOURNE.

I beg you to forgive me. My own loss is greater than yours.

GIOVANELLI, aside.

My friend the courier is a clever man!

DAISY, thoughtful a moment.

Well it's no matter.

MRS. WALKER, to Eugenio.

Please take her to her mother.

EUGENIO.

I must act at my convenience, Madame!

DAISY.

I'm not going to my mother.   Mr. Giovanelli!

GIOVANELLI, with alacrity.

Signorina?

DAISY.

Please to give me your arm.   We'll go on with our walk.

MRS. WALKER, coming between the two.

Now don't do anything dreadful!

DAISY, to Giovanelli.

Give me your arm.   (Giovanelli passes behind Mrs. Walker, and gives
Daisy his arm on the other side. She continues, with a sudden outbreak of passion.)
I see nothing dreadful but your cruel accusations!   If you
all attack me, I have a friend to defend me.

GIOVANELLI.

I will defend you always, Signorina!

MRS. WALKER.

Are you going to take her to that drinking-shop?

DAISY.

That's our own affair.   Come away, come away!

WINTERBOURNE.

I have done you a greater injury than I supposed.

DAISY.

The injury was done when you spoke to me that way!

WINTERBOURNE.

When I spoke to you?   I don't understand.

DAISY.

Half an hour ago, when you said I was so bad!

GIOVANELLI.

If people insult you, they will answer to *me*.

WINTERBOURNE, to Giovanelli.

Don't be rash, sir!   You will need all your caution.

MRS. WALKER.

High words between gentlemen, to crown the horrors!
(To Eugenio.)   Go straight and ask Mrs. Miller if she consents.

EUGENIO, smiling.

Mrs. Miller consents to everything that I approve.

DAISY.

Come away, Mr. Giovanelli!

GIOVANELLI, aside.

I shall have to take a cab!   (They walk up the stage.)

MRS. WALKER.

Mercy on us!   She is lost!

WINTERBOURNE, sternly.

Leave her alone.   She only wants a pretext!

DAISY, who has heard him, turning as she reaches the top of the stage, and
looking back a moment.

Thank you, Mr. Winterbourne!   (She goes out with Giovanelli.)

MRS. WALKER, to Winterbourne.

Yes, my dear sir, you have done a pretty piece of work.

EUGENIO, with his hands in his pockets, as at the end of the first act, watching
the scene complacently.

My little revenge on the journey to the castle!

WINTERBOURNE, looking at his watch, to himself.

Well, *I* shall have that moonlight drive!

ACT THIRD.

Rome.   Public parlors at the Hôtel de Paris ; evening.   Wide windows at the back, overlooking the Corso, open upon a balcony, which must be apparent, behind light curtains, to the audience.   The Carnival is going on outside, and the flare of torches, the sound of voices and of music, the uproar of a popular festival, come into the room, rising and falling at intervals during the whole act.

SCENE FIRST.

MRS. COSTELLO, MISS DURANT, CHARLES REVERDY.

He comes in first at the left, holding the door open for the others to follow.

REVERDY.

You can see very well from this balcony, if you won't go down into the street.

MRS. COSTELLO.

Down into the street — to be trampled to death ?   I have no desire to be butchered to make a Roman holiday.

REVERDY, aside.

They would find you a tough old morsel !   (Aloud.)   It's the last night of the Carnival, and a peculiar license prevails.

MRS. COSTELLO.

I'm happy to hear it's the last night.   Their tooting and piping and fiddling has n't stopped for a week, and my poor old head has been racked with pain.

MISS DURANT.

Is it very bad now ?   You had better go to our own quiet sitting-room, which looks out on the back.

MRS. COSTELLO.

And leave you here with this youth?

MISS DURANT.

After all — in the Carnival!

MRS. COSTELLO.

A season of peculiar license — as he himself confesses. I wonder you don't propose at once to mingle with the populace — in a fancy dress!

MISS DURANT.

I should like to very much! I'm tired of being cooped up in a balcony. If this is the last night, it's my only chance.

MRS. COSTELLO, severely.

Alice Durant, I don't recognize you! The Carnival has affected you — insidiously. You're as bad as Daisy Miller.

REVERDY.

Poor little butterfly! Don't speak harshly of *her :* she is lying ill with Roman fever.

MRS. COSTELLO.

Since her visit to the Coliseum, in the cool of the evening, with the inveterate Giovanelli?

MISS DURANT.

I suppose he'll marry her when she recovers — if she does recover!

REVERDY.

It was certainly idiotic, from the point of view of salubrity, to go to enjoy the moonlight in that particularly mouldy ruin, and the inveterate Giovanelli, who is old enough to know better, ought to have a thrashing. The poor girl may never recover. The little Flower of the West, as Mrs. Walker says, is withering on the stem. Fancy dying to the music of the Carnival!

MRS. COSTELLO.

That's the way I shall die, unless you come now and take your last look, so that we may go away and have done with it. (Goes to the window.) Good heavens, what a rabble! (Passes out on the balcony.)

REVERDY, to Miss Durant, remaining behind.

Will you give her the slip, and come out with me?

MISS DURANT, looking at him, and listening to the music.

In a fancy dress?

REVERDY.

Oh, no; simply in a mask. I've got one in my pocket. (Takes out a grotesque mask and holds it to his face a moment, shaking his head at her.) How d'ye do, lovely woman?

MISS DURANT.

Dear me, how very hideous!

REVERDY.

If *you* put it on, I shall be as handsome as ever.

MISS DURANT, aside.

If he should propose out there, it would hide my blushes!

MRS. COSTELLO, from the balcony.

Young people, what are you doing? Come out here this minute!

REVERDY.

There she is again! (Aloud.) Are you afraid they will pelt you with flowers?

MRS. COSTELLO.

A gentleman has already kissed his hand to me!

REVERDY.

A season of peculiar license! (To Miss Durant.) We can't escape from her now, but it won't be long! (They rejoin Mrs. Costello on the balcony, Reverdy holding the mask behind him. While they remain there, apparently absorbed in the spectacle in the street, Eugenio and Giovanelli come in.)

SCENE SECOND.

EUGENIO, GIOVANELLI; THEN REVERDY, MISS DURANT.

EUGENIO.

You must come in here; we can't talk in the hall.

GIOVANELLI, with a bouquet of flowers.

I have come for news of the dear young lady. I 'm terribly nervous.

EUGENIO.

You think you may lose her? It would serve you right!

GIOVANELLI.

If I lose her I shall never try again. I am passionately in love with her.

EUGENIO.

I hope so, indeed! That was part of our agreement.

GIOVANELLI.

If you begin to joke, I see she 's better.

EUGENIO.

If I begin to joke? I 'm as serious as you. If she 's better it 's no thanks to you — doing your best to kill her on my hands.

GIOVANELLI.

It was no fault of mine. She had her own way.

EUGENIO.

The Coliseum by moonlight — that was a lovely invention! Why did n't you jump into the Tiber at once?

GIOVANELLI.

We are not the first who have been there. It 's a very common excursion.

EUGENIO.

By daylight, of course; but not when the miasma rises.

GIOVANELLI.

Excuse me : it is recommended in the guide-books.

EUGENIO.

Do you make love according to Murray ? — or, perhaps, according to Baedeker ? I myself have conducted families there, to admire the general effect ; but not to spend the evening.

GIOVANELLI.

I was afraid for myself, Heaven knows !

EUGENIO.

" Afraid for yourself " is good — with an American heiress beside you !

GIOVANELLI.

I could n't induce her to come away, the moon was so bright and beautiful ! And then you wanted her to be talked about.

EUGENIO.

Yes : but I wanted you to take her alive. She 's talked about enough to-day. It was only a week ago, but the whole town knows it.

GIOVANELLI.

Per Bacco ! That solemn fool of a Winterbourne has spread the story.

EUGENIO.

The further the better ! But I thought I had given him something else to do.

GIOVANELLI.

I don't know what you had given him to do ; but, as luck would have it, he turned up at the Coliseum. He came upon us suddenly, and stood there staring. Then he took off his hat to my companion, and made her the lowest of bows.

EUGENIO.

Without a word?

GIOVANELLI.

Without a word.   He turned his back and walked off.

EUGENIO.

Stupid ass!   But it is all right: he has given her up.

GIOVANELLI.

He gave her up that day on the Pincian; he has not been near her since.

EUGENIO, aside.

The Katkoff is really perfect! — though he comes to ask about her every day.   (Aloud.)   Yes, but he wanted a reason: now he has got his reason.

GIOVANELLI, pretentiously.

I shall give him a better one than that!

EUGENIO.

He's perfectly content with this one; and it must be admitted it would suit most people.   We must hope it will suit Mr. Miller.

GIOVANELLI, gloomily.

Ah, Mr. Miller?   I seemed to see him there, too, in the moonlight!

EUGENIO.

You're afraid of him, and your fear makes images.   What did Miss Daisy do?

GIOVANELLI.

After the American had left us?   She held her tongue till we got home.

EUGENIO.

She said nothing about him?

GIOVANELLI.

Never a word, thank goodness!

EUGENIO, thoughtful a moment.

Cavaliere, you are very limited.

GIOVANELLI.

I verily believe I am, to stand here and answer your questions. All this time you have told me nothing about my adored !

EUGENIO.

She is doing very well ; it has been a light attack. She has sat up these three days, and the doctor says she needs only to be careful. But being careful doesn't suit her ; she's in despair at missing the Carnival.

GIOVANELLI, tenderly.

Enchanting young person ! Be so good as to give her these flowers. Be careful of them, you know !

EUGENIO.

I should think so — when I pay for them myself.

GIOVANELLI.

And ask if I may come up and see her.

EUGENIO, looking at the bouquet.

You get 'em handsome, I must say. — I don't know what the doctor would say to that.

GIOVANELLI, smiling.

Let me be the doctor. You'll see !

EUGENIO.

You're certainly dangerous enough for one. But you must wait till we go out — the mother and the brother and I.

GIOVANELLI.

Where are you going, at this hour ?

EUGENIO.

To show that peevish little brat the illumination.

GIOVANELLI.

Mrs. Miller leaves her daughter — at such a time ?

EUGENIO.

Master Randolph is the head of the family.

GIOVANELLI.

I must get *his* consent to the marriage, then ?

EUGENIO.

You can get it with a pound of sugar plums.

GIOVANELLI.

I 'll buy him a dozen to-morrow.

EUGENIO.

And charge them to me, of course.

GIOVANELLI, stiffly.

Please to open the door.   I 'll wait in the hall till you go out.   (Eugenio opens the door, looks at him, and then passes out first. Giovanelli follows.   When they have left the room, Reverdy and Miss Durant come in from the balcony.)

REVERDY, his finger on his lips.

Hush, hush !   She 's looking for the gentleman who kissed his hand.

MISS DURANT.

When she kissed hers back, she frightened him away !

REVERDY.

I can't stand that balcony business !   I want to dance and sing, in the midst of it, with a charming creature on my arm !

MISS DURANT.

I forbid you to touch any of your creatures !

REVERDY.

In the Carnival one may touch any one.   All common laws are suspended.

MISS DURANT.

Cousin Louisa won't listen to that.

REVERDY.

She 's a great deal worse than we herself — having an

intrigue with a perfect stranger ! Now's our chance to escape ;
before she misses us, we shall be a mile away.

MISS DURANT.

A mile away is very far! You make me feel dreadfully
like Daisy Miller.

REVERDY.

To be perfect, all you want is to be a little like her.

MISS DURANT.

Oh, you wretch — I never !

REVERDY.

There, now, you are just like her !

MISS DURANT.

I certainly am not used to being a wall-flower.

REVERDY.

A plant in a balcony is even worse. Come, come ! here's
the mask.

MISS DURANT.

It's very dreadful. I can't bear to look so ugly !

REVERDY.

Don't I know how pretty you are ?

MISS DURANT, taking his arm, aside.

He can do anything with me he wants ! (Exeunt. Enter
Daisy on the opposite side.)

SCENE THIRD.

DAISY ALONE ; THEN WINTERBOURNE, A WAITER ; MRS.
COSTELLO.

DAISY. She wears a light dressing-gown, like an invalid, and it must be apparent
that she has been ill, though this appearance must not be exaggerated. She
wanders slowly into the room, and pauses in the middle.

Ah, from here the music is very distinct — and the voices
of the crowd, and all the sound of the fête. Upstairs, in our

rooms, you can hear it just dimly. That's the way it seemed
to me — just faint and far — as I lay there with darkened
windows. It's hard to be sick when there's so much pleasure going on, especially when you're so fond of pleasure as
poor silly me! Perhaps I'm too fond; that's one of the
things I thought of as I lay there. I thought of so many —
and some of them so sad — as I listened to the far-away
Carnival. I think it was this that helped me to get better.
I was afraid I had been bad, and I wanted to live to be good
again. I was afraid I should die, and I did n't want to die.
But I'm better now, and I can walk and do everything I
want. (Listening again.) Every now and then it grows louder,
as if the people were so happy! It reminds me of that
poetry I used to learn at school, "There was a sound of
revelry by night." That's a sound I always wanted to hear.
This is the last night; and when mother and Randolph went
out, I could n't stay there alone. I waited a little; I was
afraid of meeting some one on the stairs. But every one is
in the streets, and they have gone to see the illumination.
I thought of that balcony: just to look out a little is better
than nothing. (Listens again a moment.) Every now and then it
increases. (Goes to the window, but seeing Mrs. Costello outside comes back.)
Ah, there's some one there; and with this old wrapper . . .
(Looking at her dressing-gown.) Perhaps the night air is n't good
for me; the doctor forbids the night air. Ah, what a pity
it's the last evening! (Goes to the window again, and while she stands
there a waiter throws open the door and ushers in Winterbourne, who at first does
not see her.)

THE WAITER.

The ladies are here, sir. (Surprised not to find them.) Excuse
me. I saw them come in with Mr. Reverdy, but they have
gone out again.

WINTERBOURNE.

It's not those ladies I want.   Please to ask Madame de Katkoff if she can see me.

THE WAITER.

Won't you go up to her sitting-room ?   She has a great many guests.

WINTERBOURNE, annoyed.

A great many guests ?

THE WAITER.

A party of friends, who have come to see the fête from one of her windows.   Her parlor is in the Square, and the view is even finer than from here.

WINTERBOURNE.

I know all about her parlor.   (Aside.)   It's hateful to see her with a lot of others !   (Aloud.)   Ask her if she will kindly speak to me here.

THE WAITER.

Ah, you lose a great deal, sir !   (Exit.)

WINTERBOURNE.

The servants in this place are impossible ; the young Randolph has demoralized them all !   That's the same fellow who, last summer, wanted to give me a definition of my aunt.   (Seeing Daisy.)   Ah, that poor creature !   (Aloud.) I am afraid I am intruding on you here.

DAISY, coming forward.

You have as good a right here as I.   I don't think I have any.

WINTERBOURNE.

You mean as an invalid ?   I am very happy to see you better.

DAISY.

Thank you.   I'm very well.

10

WINTERBOURNE.

I asked about you every day.

DAISY.

They never told me.

WINTERBOURNE.

That was your faithful courier!

DAISY.

He was so frightened at my illness that he could n't remember anything.

WINTERBOURNE.

Oh, yes, he was terribly afraid he should lose you. For a couple of days it was very serious.

DAISY.

How do you know that?

WINTERBOURNE.

I asked the doctor.

DAISY, aside.

He 's very strange. Why should he care?

WINTERBOURNE.

He said you had done what might kill you.

DAISY.

At the Coliseum?

WINTERBOURNE.

At the Coliseum.

DAISY.

Why did n't you tell me that, when you saw me there?

WINTERBOURNE.

Because you had an adviser in whom you have much more faith.

MISS DURANT.

Mr. Giovanelli? Oh, it 's not his fault. He begged me to come away.

WINTERBOURNE.

If you did n't mind him, you would n't have minded me.

DAISY.

I did n't care what happened. But I noticed, all the same, that you did n't speak to me.

WINTERBOURNE.

I had nothing to say.

DAISY.

You only bowed, very low.

WINTERBOURNE.

That was to express my great respect.

DAISY.

I had never had such a bow before.

WINTERBOURNE.

You had never been so worthy of it!

DAISY, aside.

He despises me! Well, I don't care! (Aloud.) It was lovely there in the moonlight.

WINTERBOURNE.

I was sure you found it so. That was another reason I did n't wish to interrupt you.

DAISY, playing indifference.

What were you doing there, all alone?

WINTERBOURNE.

I had been dining at a villa in that part of Rome, and I simply stopped, as I walked home, to take a look at the splendid ruin.

DAISY, after a pause, in the same manner.

I should n't think you 'd go round alone.

WINTERBOURNE.

I have to go as I can; I have n't your resources.

DAISY.

Don't you know any ladies?

WINTERBOURNE.

Yes; but they don't expose themselves . . .

DAISY, with quick emotion.

Expose themselves to be treated as you treated me!

WINTERBOURNE.

You are rather difficult to please.   (Reënter the waiter.)

THE WAITER.

Madame de Katkoff will come in about ten minutes, sir.

WINTERBOURNE.

Very good.
THE WAITER.

She's just pouring out tea for the company.

WINTERBOURNE.

That will do.

THE WAITER, smiling.

You know the Russians must have their tea, sir.

WINTERBOURNE.

You talk too much.

THE WAITER, going out.

He's very sharp to-night!   (Exit Waiter.)

DAISY, who has turned away a moment, coming down.

If you are expecting some one, I'll go away.

WINTERBOURNE.

There's another public room.   I'll see my friend there.

DAISY.

I have nothing to do here.   (Goes toward the door, but stops half-way, looking at him.)   You see a great deal of Madame de Kat-koff.   Does n't *she* expose herself?

WINTERBOURNE, smiling.

To dangerous consequences?   Never!

DAISY.   She comes down again, as if unable to decide to leave him.   Aside.

I 'm determined to know what he thinks.   (Aloud, in a different tone.)   I was going out on the balcony, to see what 's going on

WINTERBOURNE.

Are you not afraid of the night air?

DAISY.

I 'm not afraid of anything!

WINTERBOURNE.

Are you going to begin again?

DAISY.

Ah, I 'm too late!   It 's nearly over.   (At the moment she speaks, Mrs. Costello appears in the window, from the balcony. Reënter Mrs. Costello.)

MRS. COSTELLO, to Winterbourne.

Merciful powers!   I thought you were Mr. Reverdy! (Looking at Daisy.)   And that this young lady was my Alice!

DAISY.

Something very different, you see!   Now I can have the balcony.   (She passes out of the window.)

MRS. COSTELLO.

What are you doing with that girl?   I thought you had dropped her.

WINTERBOURNE.

I was asking about her health.   She has been down with the fever.

MRS. COSTELLO.

It will do her good — make her reflect on her sins.   But what have you done with my young companions?

WINTERBOURNE.

Nothing in the world.   The last I saw of them they were frolicking in the Corso.

MRS. COSTELLO.

Frolicking in the Corso ?   Alice and Mr. Reverdy ?

WINTERBOURNE.

I met them as I was coming from my lodgings to the hotel.   He was blowing a tin trumpet, and she was hiding behind a mask.

MRS. COSTELLO.

A tin trumpet and a mask !   Have they gone to perdition ?

WINTERBOURNE.

They are only taking advantage of the Carnival.

MRS. COSTELLO.

Taking advantage of my back ; I had turned it for three minutes !   They were on the balcony with me, looking at this vulgar riot, and they slipped away to come in here.

WINTERBOURNE.

You never give them a chance : they hunger and thirst !

MRS. COSTELLO.

A chance to masquerade ?   Think of her education !

WINTERBOURNE.

I am thinking of it now.   You see the results.

MRS. COSTELLO.

I said to myself that I was perhaps too vigilant, and I left them here a moment to talk things over.   I saw through the window a young lady and a gentleman, and I took it for granted it was they.

WINTERBOURNE.

Ingenuous aunt !   They were already a mile away !

MRS. COSTELLO.

It 's too horrible to believe.   You must immediately bring them back.

WINTERBOURNE.

Impossible just now.   I have an engagement here.

MRS. COSTELLO.

I 'll go and look for them myself!

WINTERBOURNE, laying his hand on her arm.

Don't, don't! Let them have a little fun!

MRS. COSTELLO.

I never heard of anything so cynical!

WINTERBOURNE.

Don't you want them to marry?

MRS. COSTELLO.

To marry, yes; but not to elope!

WINTERBOURNE.

Let them do it in their own way.

MRS. COSTELLO.

With a mask and a tin trumpet? A girl I 've watched like that!

WINTERBOURNE.

You have watched too much. They 'll come home engaged.

MRS. COSTELLO.

Ah, bring them, then, quickly!

WINTERBOURNE.

I will go down into the street and look; and if I see them, I will tell them what 's expected of them.

MRS. COSTELLO.

I will go to my room; I feel a headache coming on. (Before she goes out, to herself, as if a thought has struck her.) Had they bribed that monster to kiss his hand? (Exeunt.)

SCENE FOURTH.

GIOVANELLI, DAISY.

He enters the room, and she comes in from the balcony at the same moment. He advances with a radiant smile, takes both of her hands, holds them for a moment devotedly, then kisses each of them.

GIOVANELLI.

Carissima signorina! When I see you restored to health, I begin to live myself!

DAISY.

Poor old Giovanelli! I believe you *do* care for me!

GIOVANELLI.

Care for you? When I heard you were ill, I neither ate nor slept. I thought I, too, should have to have the doctor.

DAISY, laughing.

I should have sent you mine if I had known it. You must eat a good supper to-night, for I am all right now.

GIOVANELLI.

You look still a little pale.

DAISY.

I look like a fright, of course, in this dreadful dress; but I 'm only a convalescent. If I had known you were coming, I would have worn something better.

GIOVANELLI.

You look like an angel, always. You might have been sure I would come, after so many days. I was always at your door, asking for news. But now, I think, we shall never again be separated.

DAISY.

Never again? Oh, don't talk about the future! What were you doing there in the street?

GIOVANELLI.

When I looked up and saw you on the balcony, bending over like a little saint in her shrine? It was that vision that made me come up again.

DAISY.

You had gone out to enjoy the Carnival?

GIOVANELLI.

I had come here to see you; but I learned from your excellent Eugenio that your mother and your brother were going out in a carriage. They appeared at that moment, and I went down with them to the door, to wish them a happy drive. Little Randolph was greatly excited.

DAISY.

He insisted on mother's going; she 'll do anything for Randolph. But she did n't want to leave me.

GIOVANELLI, smiling.

She has left you to me!

DAISY.

Did Eugenio go with them?

GIOVANELLI.

Oh, yes; he got into the carriage. (Aside.) The cheek of that man!

DAISY.

They have left me alone, then.

GIOVANELLI.

I am almost of the family, dear Miss!

DAISY, apparently not hearing him, listening to the sounds from without.

They ought n't to have left me alone — when I 'm sick, when I 'm weak.

GIOVANELLI, anxiously.

You are not so well, then, as you say?

DAISY, looking at him a moment, with a little laugh.

You look so scared at the idea of losing me! Poor old Giovanelli! What should you do if you were to lose me?

GIOVANELLI.

Don't speak of it — it's horrible! If you are not well, you should go to your room.

DAISY.

Oh, I'm all right. I only wanted to frighten you.

GIOVANELLI.

It isn't kind — when you know how I love you!

DAISY.

I don't know it, and I don't want to know it, as I have told you often. I forbid you to speak of that.

GIOVANELLI.

You will never let me mention the future.

DAISY.

I hate the future; I care only for the present!

GIOVANELLI.

The future is the present, when one sees it as we see it.

DAISY.

I don't see it at all, and I don't want to see it. I saw it for a moment, when I was sick, and that was enough.

GIOVANELLI.

You have suffered much; but it was not my fault.

DAISY.

I don't blame you, Giovanelli. You are very kind. Where are they going, mother and Randolph?

GIOVANELLI.

Up and down the Corso; wherever there is something to see. They have an open carriage, with lots of flowers.

DAISY.

It must be charming.   Have you been going round?

GIOVANELLI.

I have strolled about a little.

DAISY.

Is it very, *very* amusing?

GIOVANELLI.

Ah, you know, I 'm an old Roman : I have seen it many times.   The illumination is better than usual, and the music is lively enough.

DAISY.

Listen to the music — listen to it!

GIOVANELLI, smiling.

You must n't let it go to your head.   (Daisy goes to the window, and stands there a moment.)   She has never been so lovely as to-night!

DAISY, coming back, with decision.

Giovanelli, you must get me a carriage.

GIOVANELLI, startled.

A carriage, signorina?

DAISY.

I must go out — I *must !*

GIOVANELLI.

There is not a carriage to be had at this hour.   Everything is taken for the fête.

DAISY.

Then I 'll go on foot.   You must take me.

GIOVANELLI.

Into the air of the night, and the crowded streets?   It 's enough to kill you!

DAISY.

It 's a lovely night, as mild as June; and it 's only for five minutes.

GIOVANELLI.

The softer the night, the greater the danger of the bad air. Five minutes, in your condition, would bring back the fever.

DAISY.

I shall have the fever if I stay here listening, longing, fidgeting ! You said I was pale; but it's only the delicacy of my complexion.

GIOVANELLI.

You are not pale now; you have a little spot in either cheek. Your mother will not be happy.

DAISY.

She should n't have left me alone, then.

GIOVANELLI.

You are not alone when you are with me.

DAISY.

Of what use are you, except to take me out?

GIOVANELLI.

It's impossible to contradict you. For five minutes, then, remember !

DAISY.

For five minutes, then; or for ten ! I 'll go and get ready. Don't mind about the carriage: we 'll do it better on foot.

GIOVANELLI, at the door.

It 's at your own risk, you know. I 'll try for a cab.

DAISY.

My own risk ! I 'm not afraid.

GIOVANELLI, kissing his hand to her.

You are awfully beautiful ! (Exit Giovanelli.)

DAISY, alone.

I 'm not afraid — I don't care ! I don't like him to-night; he 's too serious. I would rather be out-of-doors

with him than shut up here. Poor Giovanelli; if he thinks
I love him, after all I 've said to the contrary . . . I can
dress in three minutes. (She is going to the door opposite to the one
through which Giovanelli has made his exit when Madame de Katkoff comes in,
meeting her.)

SCENE FIFTH.

DAISY, MADAME DE KATKOFF.

They stand a moment, looking at each other.

MADAME DE KATKOFF, very kindly.

I have not the pleasure of knowing you, though we have
spent half the winter in the same hotel; but I have heard of
your illness, and you must let me tell you how glad I am to
see you better.

DAISY, aside.

Why does she speak to me? I don't like her, nor want
to know her. (Aloud.) Thank you, I 'm better. I 'm going
out.

MADAME DE KATKOFF.

You must be better, indeed; but (with interest) you look a
little flushed.

DAISY.

It 's talking with a stranger. I think I must go.

MADAME DE KATKOFF.

Perhaps you can tell me something first. A gentleman
sent me his name, and I was told I should find him here.
May I ask you whether you have seen such a person?

DAISY.

If you mean Mr. Winterbourne, he was here just now;
but he went away with his aunt.

MADAME DE KATKOFF.

I suppose he 'll come back, then. But he ought n't to keep me waiting.

DAISY, very coldly.

I have n't the least idea what he ought to do. I know nothing whatever of his movements.

MADAME DE KATKOFF, aside.

Poor little thing, she hates me! But she does n't hate *him*. (Aloud.) I 'm a stranger as you say; but I should be very glad to become a little less of one.

DAISY.

Why should you want to know me? I 'm not of your age.

MADAME DE KATKOFF, aside, smiling.

She hates me indeed! (Aloud.) I should be tempted to say that we might know each other a little as mother and daughter — if I had n't heard that you are already the devoted daughter of a devoted mother.

DAISY.

She 's good enough for me — and I 'm good enough for her.

MADAME DE KATKOFF, more and more gracious.

I envy you both, and I am happy to have the opportunity of saying so. One does n't know how pretty you are till one talks to you.

DAISY.

If you are laughing at my dress, I am just going to change it.

MADAME DE KATKOFF.

Laughing at your dress? It has always been my admiration.

DAISY, aside.

What does she mean by that? It 's not as good as hers. (Aloud.) I can't stay with you. I 'm going to the Carnival.

MADAME DE KATKOFF.

It will last all night; you have plenty of time. I have heard Mr. Winterbourne speak of you.

DAISY.

I did n't suppose he ever did that.

MADAME DE KATKOFF.

Oh! very often. That 's why I want to know you.

DAISY.

It 's a strange reason. He must have told you pretty things of me.

MADAME DE KATKOFF.

He has told me you 're a charming young girl.

DAISY, aside.

Oh, what an awful story! (Aloud.) I don't understand what you want of me.

MADAME DE KATKOFF, aside.

I can hardly tell her that I want to make up to her for the harm I have done her, for I can't do that unless I give up everything. (Aloud, as if struck by an idea.) I want to be kind to you. I want to keep you from going out.

DAISY, smiling.

I don't think you can do that.

MADAME DE KATKOFF.

You are barely convalescent : you must n't expose yourself.

DAISY.

It won't hurt any one but me.

MADAME DE KATKOFF.

We all take a great interest in you. We should be in despair if you were to have a relapse.

DAISY.

You all despise me and think me dreadful; that 's what you all do!

MADAME DE KATKOFF.

Where did you learn that remarkable fact?

DAISY.

Mr. Winterbourne told me — since you speak of Mr. Winterbourne.

MADAME DE KATKOFF.

I don't think you understood him. Mr. Winterbourne is a perfect gentleman.

DAISY.

Have you come here to praise him to me? That's strange — for you!

MADAME DE KATKOFF.

You know at least that I consider him an excellent friend.

DAISY.

I know nothing whatever about it. (Aside.) She wants to torture me — to triumph!

MADAME DE KATKOFF, aside.

She's as proud as she is pretty! (Aloud.) Are you going out alone?

DAISY.

No, indeed, I have a friend.

MADAME DE KATKOFF, aside.

A friend as well as I. (Aloud.) My dear child, I am very sorry for you. You have too many wrong ideas.

DAISY.

That's exactly what they say!

MADAME DE KATKOFF.

I don't mean it as other people may have meant it. You make a great many mistakes.

DAISY.

As many as I possibly can! In America I was always right.

MADAME DE KATKOFF.

Try and believe you are in America now. I'm not an American, but I want to be your friend.

DAISY.

I'm much obliged to you, but I don't trust you.

MADAME DE KATKOFF.

You trust the wrong people. With whom are you going out?

DAISY.

I don't think I'm obliged to tell you.

MADAME DE KATKOFF, gently.

I ask for a very good motive.

DAISY, aside.

She may be better than I think. (Aloud.) With Mr. Giovanelli.

MADAME DE KATKOFF, smiling.

A mysterious Italian — introduced by your courier!

DAISY, with simplicity.

Oh, no; Eugenio got some one else!

MADAME DE KATKOFF, aside.

Adorable innocence! (Aloud.) That's all I wanted to know.

DAISY.

I hope you have nothing to say against him.

MADAME DE KATKOFF.

Nothing but this : he's not a gentleman.

DAISY.

Not a gentleman? Poor old Giovanelli!

MADAME DE KATKOFF, aside.

"Poor old Giovanelli?" Good! (Aloud.) If he were a gentleman, he wouldn't ask you to do what you tell me you are on the point of doing.

11

DAISY.

He never asked me.   He does what I wish!

MADAME DE KATKOFF, aside.

She does n't care a fig for him — and I should like to exasperate the courier.   (Aloud.)   It's none of my business; but why do you wish, in your condition, to go out?

DAISY.

Because it's the last night of the Carnival, and I have no one else to take me.

MADAME DE KATKOFF.

Excuse me; but where is your mother?

DAISY.

Gone out with my brother.

MADAME DE KATKOFF, aside.

Extraordinary family!   (Aloud.)   Let me make you an offer: I will order out my carriage, and take you myself.

DAISY, staring.

Take me yourself?   (Then abruptly, ironically.)   Pray, what would become of Mr. Winterbourne?

MADAME DE KATKOFF, aside.

She adores him!   (Aloud.)   Ah, you don't care for Giovanelli!

DAISY.

Whether I care for him or not, I must n't keep him waiting.   (Exit Daisy, hastily.)

MADAME DE KATKOFF, alone.

She's trembling with agitation, and her poor little heart is full.   She thought I wished to torment her.   My position is odiously false!   And to think I hold her happiness in my hands!   (Winterbourne comes in.)   His, too, poor fellow!   Ah, I can't hold it any longer!

SCENE SIXTH.

MADAME DE KATKOFF, WINTERBOURNE.

WINTERBOURNE.

I am afraid I have kept you waiting.   I was carried away by my aunt.

MADAME DE KATKOFF.

Is she keeping the Carnival, your aunt?

WINTERBOURNE.

No, but her companions are.   They are masquerading in the Corso, and she's in despair.   She sent me to hunt them up, but they are lost in the crowd.

MADAME DE KATKOFF.

Do you mean the young lady whom you described as so prim?   If that's a specimen of her primness, I was right in my little theory.

WINTERBOURNE.

Your little theory?

MADAME DE KATKOFF.

That the grave ones are the gay ones.

WINTERBOURNE.

Poor Miss Durant isn't gay: she's simply desperate. My aunt keeps such watch at the door that she has been obliged to jump out of the window. — Have you waited very long?

MADAME DE KATKOFF.

I hardly know.   I have had company — Miss Daisy Miller!

WINTERBOURNE.

That must have made the time fly!

MADAME DE KATKOFF.

She is very touching.

WINTERBOURNE.

Very, indeed.   She has gone to pieces.

MADAME DE KATKOFF.

Gone to pieces?

WINTERBOURNE.

She's quite impossible.   You ought n't to talk to her.

MADAME DE KATKOFF, aside.

Ah, what a fool I have made of him! (Aloud.)   You think
she will corrupt my innocence?

WINTERBOURNE, after a moment.

I don't like you to speak of her.   Please don't.

MADAME DE KATKOFF.

She completes my little theory — that the gay ones are
the grave ones.

WINTERBOURNE.

If she's grave, she well may be: her situation is intensely
grave.   As for her native solemnity, you used to insist upon
that when, for reasons best known to yourself, you conceived
the remarkable design of inducing me to make love to her.
You dropped the idea as suddenly as you took it up; but I
am very sorry to see any symptoms of your taking it up
again.   It seems to me it's hardly the moment.

MADAME DE KATKOFF, aside.

It's more the moment than you think.

WINTERBOURNE, rather harshly.

I was very sorry to learn, on coming here, that you have
your rooms full of people.

MADAME DE KATKOFF.

They have come to look out of my windows.   It is not
my fault that I have such a view of the Corso.

WINTERBOURNE.

You had given me to understand that we should be alone.

MADAME DE KATKOFF.

I did n't ask them ; they came themselves.

WINTERBOURNE, impatiently.

I wish to heaven they had stayed at home !

MADAME DE KATKOFF.

Should you like me to turn them out ?

WINTERBOURNE.

I should like it particularly.

MADAME DE KATKOFF.

The ambassador and all ?

WINTERBOURNE.

You told me a month ago that where I was concerned you did n't care a straw for the ambassador.

MADAME DE KATKOFF, after a moment.

A month ago — yes !

WINTERBOURNE.

If you intended to change so soon, you ought to have notified me at the moment.

MADAME DE KATKOFF.

The ambassador is very considerate.   When I have a few visitors, he helps me to entertain them.

WINTERBOURNE.

That proves how little you have need of me.

MADAME DE KATKOFF.

I have left my guests in his charge, with perfect confidence.

WINTERBOURNE.

Oh, if you mean you are at liberty, that 's just what I want.

MADAME DE KATKOFF.

What does it occur to you to propose?

WINTERBOURNE.

That you should drive out with me, to see the illumination.

MADAME DE KATKOFF.

I have seen fifty illuminations! I am sick of the
Carnival.

WINTERBOURNE.

It is n't the Carnival; it 's the drive. I have a carriage
at the door.

MADAME DE KATKOFF.

I have no doubt it would be charming; but I am not at
liberty in that sense. I can't leave a roomful of people
planted there! I really don't see why they should make
you so savage.

WINTERBOURNE.

I am not savage, but I am disappointed. I counted on
this evening: it 's a week since we have been alone.

MADAME DE KATKOFF.

Do I appear to so little advantage in company? Are you
ashamed of me when others are present? I do the best
I can.

WINTERBOURNE.

You were always strange — and you always will be!
Sometimes I think you have taken a vow to torment me.

MADAME DE KATKOFF.

I have taken a vow — that 's very true; and I admit I
am strange. We Russians are, you know: you had warning
of that!

WINTERBOURNE.

Yes; but you abuse the national privilege. I am never
safe with you — never sure of you. You turn from one
thing to the other.

MADAME DE KATKOFF, aside.

Poor fellow, he 's bewildered! (Aloud.) Will you do me a favor?

WINTERBOURNE.

I am sure it 's something horrible!

MADAME DE KATKOFF.

You say you have a carriage at the door. Take it, and go after that poor girl.

WINTERBOURNE.

Oh, are you coming back to *her?* You try my patience!

MADAME DE KATKOFF.

She has just risen from an attack of fever, and it strikes her as a knowing thing to finish her evening in the streets!

WINTERBOURNE, starting a little.

She has gone out — looking that way?

MADAME DE KATKOFF, aside.

That will touch him! (Aloud.) She won't come home alive.

WINTERBOURNE, attentive.

Do you believe that?

MADAME DE KATKOFF, aside.

It *has* touched him! (Aloud.) I think it 's madness. Her only safety was to have left Rome the moment she could be moved.

WINTERBOURNE, after a pause.

I am not sure the best thing that can happen to her is not to die! She ought to perish in her flower, as she once said to me!

MADAME DE KATKOFF.

That 's a convenient theory, to save you the trouble of a drive!

WINTERBOURNE.

You are remarkably pressing, but you had better spare your sarcasm. I have no further interest in the fate of Miss Daisy Miller, and no commission whatever to interfere with her movements. She has a mother — in disguise — and she has other protectors. I don't suppose she has gone out alone.

MADAME DE KATKOFF.

She has gone with her Italian.

WINTERBOURNE.

Giovanelli? Ah, the scoundrel!

MADAME DE KATKOFF, smiling, aside.

My dear friend, you are all right. (Aloud.) Gently, gently! It's not *his* fault.

WINTERBOURNE.

That she is infatuated? Perhaps not.

MADAME DE KATKOFF.

Infatuated? She does n't care a straw for him!

WINTERBOURNE.

And to prove her indifference, she lets him take her on this devil's drive? I don't quite see it.

MADAME DE KATKOFF.

He's her convenience — her little pretext — her poor old Giovanelli. He fetches and carries, and she finds him very useful; but that's the end of it. She takes him to drive: he does n't take her.

WINTERBOURNE.

Did she kindly inform you of these interesting facts?

MADAME DE KATKOFF.

I had a long talk with her. One woman understands another!

WINTERBOURNE.

I hope she understands you.   It's more than I do.

MADAME DE KATKOFF.

She has gone out because she's unhappy.   She doesn't care what becomes of her.

WINTERBOURNE.

I never suspected her of such tragic propensities.   Pray, what is she unhappy about?

MADAME DE KATKOFF.

About the hard things people say of her.

WINTERBOURNE.

She has only to behave like other girls, then.

MADAME DE KATKOFF.

Like your friend, Miss Durant?   A pretty model, this evening!   You say you hope poor Daisy understands me; but she does n't — and that's part of the misery.   She can't make out what I have made of you!

WINTERBOURNE.

A creature as miserable as herself!   You might have explained : you had the opportunity.

MADAME DE KATKOFF.

She left me abruptly — and I lost it forever!

WINTERBOURNE.

All this is nothing to *us*.   When will your friends leave you?

MADAME DE KATKOFF, after a pause.

No, it's nothing to us. — I have n't asked my friends how long they mean to stay.

WINTERBOURNE.

Till eleven o'clock — till twelve?

MADAME DE KATKOFF.

Till one in the morning, perhaps — or till two. They will see the Carnival out. (Smiling.) You had much better join us!

WINTERBOURNE, passionately.

Unfathomable woman! In pity's name, what did you mean by raising my hopes to such a point, a month ago, only to dash them to the ground?

MADAME DE KATKOFF.

I tried to make you happy — but I did n't succeed.

WINTERBOURNE.

You tried? Are you trying now?

MADAME DE KATKOFF.

No, I have given it up: it 's a waste of time!

WINTERBOURNE.

Have you forgotten the day on the Pincian, after your arrival, and what you suddenly offered me — what you promised me — there? You had kept me at arm's length for three years, and suddenly the barrier dropped. The angel of justice has kept the record of my gratitude and eagerness — as well as of my surprise; and if my tenderness and respect were not greater than ever, it is because you had already had the best of them! Have you forgotten our moonlight drive through the streets of Rome, with its rich confusion of ancient memories and new-born hopes? You were perfect that evening, and for many days afterwards. But suddenly you began to change — to be absent, to be silent, to be cold, to go back to your old attitude. To-night it 's as if you were trying to make me angry! Do you wish to throw me over, and leave me lying in the dust? Are you only the most audacious of coquettes?

MADAME DE KATKOFF.

It's not I who have changed; it's you! Of course I remember our moonlight drive, and how glad you were to take it. You were happy for an hour — you were happy for three days. There were novelty and excitement in finding that, after all, I had a heart in my bosom; and for a moment the discovery amused you. But only for a moment! So long as I refused to listen to you, you cared for me. From the day I yielded, I became a bore!

WINTERBOURNE.

If you want to get rid of me, don't put it off on *me!*

MADAME DE KATKOFF.

You don't really care for me; your heart is somewhere else. You are too proud to confess it, but your love for me is an elaborate deception.

WINTERBOURNE.

The deception is yours, then — not mine!

MADAME DE KATKOFF.

You are restless, discontented, unhappy. You are sore and sick at heart, and you have tried to forget it in persuading yourself that *I* can cure your pain. I *can* cure it; but not by encouraging your illusion!

WINTERBOURNE.

If you thought it an illusion, why did you turn there and smile on me?

MADAME DE KATKOFF.

Because I was vile and wicked — because I have played a part and worn a mask, like those idiots in the Carnival — because I am a most unhappy woman!

WINTERBOURNE, looking at her, surprised.

I assure you, I understand you less and less!

MADAME DE KATKOFF.

I had an end to gain, and I thought it precious; but I have suddenly begun to loathe it! When I met that poor girl just now, and looked into her face, I was filled with compassion and shame. She is dying, I say, and between us we are killing her! Dying because she loves you, and because she thinks you despise her! Dying because you have turned away from her, and she has tried to stifle the pang! Dying because I have held you here — under compulsion of a scoundrel — and she thinks she has lost you forever! I read it all in her eyes — the purest I ever saw. I am sick of the ghastly comedy, and I must tell the miserable truth. If you will believe me, it's not too late!

WINTERBOURNE, amazed and bewildered.

Under compulsion — of a scoundrel?

MADAME DE KATKOFF.

I have the misfortune to be in the clutches of one, and so has our little friend. You know that her mother's horrible courier was once in my husband's service. Thanks to that accident, he has some papers of mine which I wish to buy back. To make me pay for them, he has forced me to play his game.

WINTERBOURNE.

His game? What has he to do with a game?

MADAME DE KATKOFF.

I don't defend him: I explain. He has selected a husband for his young lady, and your superior attractions had somehow to be muffled up. You were to be kept out of the way.

WINTERBOURNE, frowning.

Because I love her? (Correcting himself.) I mean, because he thinks so.

MADAME DE KATKOFF, smiling.

You see I am right! Because *she* loves you: he has discovered that! So he had the happy thought of saying to me, "Keep Mr. Winterbourne employed, and if the young lady marries my candidate you shall have your letter."

WINTERBOURNE.

Your letter? What letter?

MADAME DE KATKOFF.

A very silly — but very innocent — one that I wrote some ten years ago.

WINTERBOURNE.

Why did n't you ask me to get it?

MADAME DE KATKOFF.

Because I did n't want it enough for that; and now I don't want it all.

WINTERBOURNE.

You shall have it — I promise you that.

MADAME DE KATKOFF.

You are very generous, after the trick I have played you.

WINTERBOURNE.

The trick? Was it *all* a trick?

MADAME DE KATKOFF.

An infamous, pitiless trick! I was frightened, I was tempted, I was demoralized; he had me in his power. To be cruel to you was bad enough: to be cruel to her was a crime I shall try to expiate!

WINTERBOURNE, seated, his head in his hands.

You will excuse me if I feel rather stunned.

MADAME DE KATKOFF, sinking on her knees.

I ask your forgiveness! I have been living in a bad dream.

WINTERBOURNE.

Ah, you have hurt me — more than I can say !

MADAME DE KATKOFF, rising to her feet.

Don't think of yourself — think of her ! If I had only met her before, how much sooner *I* should have done that ! We will go and find her together ; we will bring her back ; we will nurse her and comfort her, and make her understand !

WINTERBOURNE.

It's all so extraordinary — and I have only your word for it.

MADAME DE KATKOFF.

See if she contradicts me when you tell her you love her ! You don't venture to deny that.

WINTERBOURNE.

I have denied it to myself : why should n't I deny it to you ?

MADAME DE KATKOFF.

You have denied it to yourself ? Who, then, had charged you with it ?

WINTERBOURNE.

You are not consistent, but you are perhaps more consistent than I. And you are very deep !

MADAME DE KATKOFF.

I am deep enough to be very sure that from this moment forward I shall be nothing to you. If I have cured you of a baseless passion, that at least is a good work. Venture to say that for these three weeks I have satisfied you.

WINTERBOURNE, turning away.

You are pitiless — you are terrible !

MADAME DE KATKOFF, looking at him a moment.

My vanity bleeds : be that my penance ! Don't lose time. Go to her now.

WINTERBOURNE, in thought, gloomily.

Dying ? — Dying ? — Dying ?

MADAME DE KATKOFF.

That was a little for the sake of argument. She will live again — for you !

WINTERBOURNE, in the same tone.

Gone out with that man ? Always with him !

MADAME DE KATKOFF.

My dear friend, she has her little pride, as well as you She pretends to flirt with Giovanelli becàuse her poor, swollen heart whispers to her to be brave !

WINTERBOURNE, uncertain.

Pretends — only pretends ?

MADAME DE KATKOFF, impatient.

Oh, you have been stupid ; but be clever now !

WINTERBOURNE, after a pause.

How am I to know that this is not another trick ?

MADAME DE KATKOFF, clasping her hands, but smiling.

Have mercy on me ! Those words are my punishment !

WINTERBOURNE.

I have been an idiot — I have been a brute — I have been a butcher !

MADAME DE KATKOFF.

Perhaps she has come back. For God's sake, go and see !

WINTERBOURNE.

And if she is still out there ? I can't talk of these things in the street.

MADAME DE KATKOFF.

Bring her home, bring her home ! Every moment 's a danger. I offered to go with you ; but you would rather go alone

WINTERBOURNE, takes up his hat.

Yes, I would rather go alone. You have hurt me very much; but you shall have your letter.

MADAME DE KATKOFF.

I don't care for my letter now. There's such a weight off my heart that I don't feel that one. (She leaves the room by the right, and Winterbourne is on the point of quitting it on the other side, when Mrs. Walker, Miss Durant, and Charles Reverdy come in, meeting him.)

SCENE SEVENTH.

WINTERBOURNE, MRS. WALKER, MISS DURANT, REVERDY.

MRS. WALKER.

Pray, where is your aunt, Mr. Winterbourne? I have brought her back her truants.

WINTERBOURNE.

She has retired to her room, to nurse a headache produced by the sudden collapse of her illusions.

MISS DURANT.

I thought she would be rather shocked; but Mr. Reverdy assured me that in the Carnival all common laws are suspended.

REVERDY.

So we thought the law that governs Mrs. Costello's headaches might conform to the others.

WINTERBOURNE.

What did you think about the law that governs her temper?

REVERDY.

Nothing at all, because, so far as I have ascertained, there is n't any!

MRS. WALKER, to Winterbourne.

They were jostling along, arm in arm, in the midst of the excited populace.   I saw them from my carriage, and, having the Consul with me, I immediately overhauled them.   The young lady had a wonderful disguise, but I recognized her from Mr. Reverdy's manner.

MISS DURANT.

There, sir, I told you you had too much !

REVERDY, aside.

One needs a good deal, when one 's about to make an offer of one 's heart.   (Aloud.)   It takes a vast deal of manner to carry off a tin trumpet !   (Winterbourne has listened to this absently; he appears restless and preoccupied ; walks up, and goes out upon the balcony.)

MRS. WALKER, noticing Winterbourne.

What 's the matter with him ? — All I can say is that in my representative position I thought I must interfere.

REVERDY, aside.

The wife of the Consul again ?   Our consuls ought to be bachelors !

MRS. WALKER.

You were dragging her along, with your arm placed as if you were waltzing.

REVERDY.

That 's very true ; we were just trying a few rounds.

MRS. WALKER.

In that dense mass of people, where you were packed like sardines ?

REVERDY.

We were all turning together; it was all one waltz !

MRS. WALKER, to Miss Durant.

Mrs. Costello, my dear, will make you dance in earnest !

12

MISS DURANT.

I don't care for Mrs. Costello now!

REVERDY.

Let me thank you for those noble words. (Aside.) You understood, then?

MISS DURANT, ingenuous.

Understood what?

REVERDY.

What I was saying when she came down on us.

MISS DURANT.

Oh yes, as far as you had gone!

REVERDY.

I must go a little farther.

MRS. WALKER, who has gone up to Winterbourne, and comes down with him.

You may be interested to hear that I saw our little friend in the crowd.

WINTERBOURNE.

Our little friend?

MRS. WALKER.

Whom we tried to save from drowning. I did n't try this time.

WINTERBOURNE.

In the crowd, on foot?

MRS. WALKER.

In the thickest and roughest part of it, on Giovanelli's arm. The crush was so dense, it was enough to kill her.

MISS DURANT.

They are very good-natured, but you *do* suffocate!

MRS. WALKER.

She 'll suffocate easily, in her weak state.

WINTERBOURNE.

Oh, I can't stand this! Excuse me. (Exit Winterbourne.)

MRS. WALKER.

What's the matter with him, I should like to know?

MISS DURANT.

He has been like that these three weeks, rushing in and out — always in a fidget.

REVERDY, to Mrs. Walker.

He's in love with Miss Durant, and he can't stand the spectacle of our mutual attachment.

MISS DURANT, gayly.

You horrid vain creature! If that's all that troubles him!

REVERDY, aside.

She'll accept me! (Aloud.) Courage — the old lady! (Enter Mrs. Costello.)

SCENE EIGHTH.

MRS. WALKER, MISS DURANT, REVERDY, MRS. COSTELLO; THEN DAISY, WINTERBOURNE, GIOVANELLI, MADAME DE KATKOFF.

MRS. COSTELLO. (She stops a moment, looking sternly from Miss Durant to Reverdy.)

Alice Durant, have you forgotten your education?

MISS DURANT.

Dear Cousin Louisa, my education made no provision for the Carnival!

REVERDY.

That's not in the regular course; it's one of the extras.

MISS DURANT.

I was just going to your room, to tell you we had come back.

MRS. COSTELLO.

I have passed an hour there, in horrible torture.   I could stand it no longer: I came to see if, for very shame, you had n't reappeared.

MRS. WALKER.

The Consul and I picked them up, and made them get into our carriage.   So you see it was not for shame!

REVERDY.

It was n't for ours, at least ; it was for yours.

MRS. COSTELLO, with majesty, to Miss Durant.

We shall start for America to-morrow.

MISS DURANT.

I am delighted to hear it.   There, at least, we can walk about.

MRS. COSTELLO.

Ah, but you will find no Carnival !

REVERDY.

My dear Madam, we shall make our own.

MRS. COSTELLO, aside to Miss Durant.

This time, it 's to be hoped, he has done it ?

MISS DURANT, blushing and looking down.

He was on the very point, when Mrs. Walker interrupted.

MRS. COSTELLO.

I declare, it 's beyond a joke — to take you back just as I brought you.

MISS DURANT.

It 's very tiresome ; but it 's not my fault.

REVERDY, who has been talking to Mrs. Walker

Miss Alice, shall we try the balcony again ?

MRS. COSTELLO.

It 's past midnight, if you please ; time for us all to retire.

REVERDY.

That's just what I propose : to retire to the balcony!

MISS DURANT, to Mrs. Costello.

Just occupy Mrs. Walker!

REVERDY, to Mrs. Walker.

Just keep hold of Mrs. Costello! (Offers his arm to Miss Durant, and leads her to the balcony.)

MRS. WALKER, looking after them.

I must wait till the Consul comes. My dear friend, I hope those young people are engaged.

MRS. COSTELLO, with asperity.

They might be, if it had n't been for you!

MRS. WALKER, surprised.

Pray, how have I prevented ? . . .

MRS. COSTELLO.

You interrupted Mr. Reverdy, just now, in the very middle . . .

MRS. WALKER.

The middle of a declaration? I thought it was a jig! (As the door of the room is flung open.) Bless my soul! what's this? (Enter rapidly Winterbourne, carrying Daisy, in a swoon, in his arms, and followed by Giovanelli, who looks both extremely alarmed and extremely indignant. At the same moment Madame de Katkoff enters from the opposite side.)

MADAME DE KATKOFF, with a cry.

Ah, it's all over! She is gone!

WINTERBOURNE.

A chair! A chair! Heaven forgive us, she is dying! (Giovanelli has quickly pushed forward a large arm-chair, in which Winterbourne places Daisy with great tenderness. She lies there motionless and unconscious. The others gather round. Miss Durant and Reverdy come in from the balcony.)

MRS. COSTELLO, seeing the two last.

Ah, they 're interrupted again!

MRS. WALKER.

This time, she's really drowned!

GIOVANELLI, much agitated, but smiling to Mrs. Costello and Mrs. Walker.

It will pass in a moment. It is only the effect of the crowd — the pressure of the mob!

WINTERBOURNE, beside Daisy, with passionate tenderness.

It will pass — because *she's* passing! Dead — dead — in my arms!

MRS. COSTELLO, harshly.

A pretty place for her to be! She'll come to life again: they don't die like that.

MRS. WALKER, indignant, to Giovanelli.

The pressure of the mob? A proper pressure — for a little Flower!

GIOVANELLI, bewildered and apologetic.

She was so lovely that they all made way; but just near the hotel we encountered one of those enormous cars, laden with musicians and maskers. The crowd was driven back, and we were hustled and smothered. She gave a little cry, and before I knew it she had fainted. The next moment this gentleman — by I know not what warrant — had taken her in his arms.

WINTERBOURNE.

By the warrant of being her countryman! Instead of entertaining those ladies, you had better go for a doctor.

GIOVANELLI.

They have sent from the hotel. Half a dozen messengers started.

REVERDY.

Half a dozen is no one at all! I will go and bring one myself — in five minutes.

MISS DURANT.

Go, go, my dear! I give you leave. (Reverdy hurries out.)

MRS. COSTELLO, to Miss Durant.

"My dear, my dear"? Has he done it, then?

MISS DURANT.

Oh yes, we just managed it. (Looking at Daisy.) Poor little thing!

MRS. COSTELLO.

Ah, *she* has n't a husband!

WINTERBOURNE, angry, desperate, to the others.

Can't you do something? Can't you speak to her? — can't you help her?

MRS. WALKER.

I will do anything in the world! I will go for the Consul. (She hurries away on the right.)

MRS. COSTELLO.

I have something in my room — a precious elixir, that I use for my headaches. (To Miss Durant.) But I 'll not leave *you!*

MISS DURANT.

Not even now?

MRS. COSTELLO.

Not till you are married! (They depart on the left.)

WINTERBOURNE, holding Daisy's hands and looking into her face·

Daisy! — Daisy! — *Daisy!*

MADAME DE KATKOFF, who all this time has been kneeling on the other side of her, her face buried on the arm of the chair, in the attitude of a person weeping.

If she can hear that, my friend, she 's saved! (To Daisy, appealing.) My child, my child, we have wronged you, but we love you!

WINTERBOURNE, in the same manner.

Daisy, my dearest, my darling! Wake a moment, if only to forgive me!

MADAME DE KATKOFF.

She moves a little! (Aside, rising to her feet.) He never spoke so to me!

GIOVANELLI, a little apart, looking round him.

Where is he, where is he — that ruffian Eugenio ?

WINTERBOURNE.

In the name of pity, has no one gone for her mother? (To Giovanelli.) Don't stand there, sir! Go for her mother!

GIOVANELLI, angrily.

Give your commands to some one else! It is not for me to do your errands.

MADAME DE KATKOFF, going to him pleadingly.

Have n't you common compassion? Do you want to see the child die?

GIOVANELLI, folding his arms.

I would rather see her die than live to be his!

WINTERBOURNE.

There is little hope of her being mine. I have insulted — I have defamed — her innocence!

GIOVANELLI.

Ay, speak of her innocence! Her innocence was divine!

DAISY, stirring and murmuring.

Mother!   Mother!

WINTERBOURNE.

She lives, she lives, and she shall choose between us!

GIOVANELLI.

Ah, when I hear *her* voice, I obey! (Exit.)

DAISY, slowly opening her eyes.

Where am I?   Where have I been?

MADAME DE KATKOFF.

She 's saved!   She 's saved!

WINTERBOURNE.

You are with me, little Daisy.   With me forever!

MADAME DE KATKOFF.

Ah, decidedly I had better leave you !   (Goes out to the balcony.)

DAISY, looking at Winterbourne.

With you ?   With *you ?*   What has happened ?

WINTERBOURNE, still on his knees beside her.

Something very blessed.   I understand you — I love you !

DAISY, gazing at him a moment.

Oh, I'm very happy !   (Sinks back again, closing her eyes.)

WINTERBOURNE.

We shall be happy together when you have told me you forgive me.   Let me hear you say it — only three words ! (He waits. She remains silent.)   Ah, she sinks away again ! Daisy, won't you live — won't you live for *me ?*

DAISY, murmuring.

It was all for you — it was all for you !

WINTERBOURNE, burying his head in her lap.

Vile idiot !   Impenetrable fool !

DAISY, with her eyes still closed.

I shall be better — but you must n't leave me.

WINTERBOURNE.

Never again, Daisy — never again !   (At this moment Eugenio strides into the room by the door opposite to the one through which Giovanelli has gone out.)

———————

SCENE NINTH.

WINTERBOURNE, DAISY, EUGENIO, MADAME DE KAT-
KOFF; THEN RANDOLPH, AND ALL THE OTHERS.

EUGENIO, looking amazed at Daisy and Winterbourne.

What does this mean ?   What horrible thing has happened ?

WINTERBOURNE, on his feet.

You will learn what has happened quite soon enough to please you ! But in the meanwhile, it is decent that this young lady should see her mother. (While he speaks, Madame de Katkoff comes back and takes her place at Daisy's side, where she stands with her eyes fixed upon Eugenio.)

EUGENIO.

Her mother is not important : Miss Miller is in my care. *Cara signorina*, do you suffer ?

DAISY, vaguely.

Poor mother, poor mother ! She has gone to the Carnival.

EUGENIO.

She came home half an hour ago. She has gone to bed.

MADAME DE KATKOFF.

Don't you think there would be a certain propriety in your requesting her to get up ? (Randolph comes in at this moment, hearing Madame de Katkoff's words.)

RANDOLPH.

She *is* getting up, you can bet your life ! She 's going to give it to Daisy.

MADAME DE KATKOFF.

Come and speak to your sister. She has been very ill. (She draws Randolph towards her, and keeps him near her.)

DAISY, smiling languidly at her brother.

You are up very late — very late.

RANDOLPH.

I can't sleep — over here ! I 've been talking to that waiter.

EUGENIO, anxious.

I don't see the Cavaliere. Where is he gone ?

RANDOLPH.

He came up to tell mother, and I came back ahead of him. (To Giovanelli, who at this moment returns.) Hallo, Cavaliere !

GIOVANELLI, solemnly, coming in.

Mrs. Miller is dressing.   She will presently arrive.

MADAME DE KATKOFF, to Randolph.

Go and help your mother, and tell her your sister is better.

RANDOLPH.

I 'll tell her through the door — or she 'll put me to bed ! (Marches away.)

GIOVANELLI, approaching Eugenio, aside.

I shall never have the girl !

EUGENIO.

You had better have killed her !   (Aside.)   He shall pay me for his flowers !   (Reënter Reverdy.)

REVERDY.

The doctor will be here in five minutes.

MADAME DE KATKOFF.

He will not be necessary now ; nor even (seeing Mrs. Costello come back with a little bottle, and accompanied by Miss Durant) this lady's precious elixir !

MRS. COSTELLO, approaching Daisy, rather stiffly.

Perhaps you would like to hold it to your nose.

DAISY, takes the phial, looking at Mrs. Costello with a little smile.

Well, I was bound you should speak to me !

REVERDY.

And without a presentation, after all !

WINTERBOURNE.

Oh yes, I must present.   (To his aunt.)   I present you my wife !

GIOVANELLI, starting ; then recovering himself and folding his arms.

I congratulate you, Mademoiselle, on your taste for the unexpected.

DAISY.

Well, it *is* unexpected.   But I never deceived you!

GIOVANELLI.

Oh, no, you have n't deceived me :   you have only ruined me!

DAISY.

Poor old Giovanelli !   Well, you 've had a good time.

MRS. COSTELLO, impressively, to Winterbourne.

Your wife ?

WINTERBOURNE.

My dear aunt, she *has* stood the test !

EUGENIO, who has walked round to Madame de Katkoff, in a low tone.

You have n't kept the terms of our bargain.

MADAME DE KATKOFF.

I am sick of your bargain — and of you !

EUGENIO.   (He eyes her a moment; then, vindictively.)

I shall give your letter to Mr. Winterbourne.

MADAME DE KATKOFF.

Coward !   (Aside, joyously.)   And Mr. Winterbourne will give it to me.

GIOVANELLI, beside Eugenio.

You must find me another heiress.

EUGENIO.

I thought you said you had had enough.

GIOVANELLI.

I have been thinking over my debts.

EUGENIO.

We will see, then, with my next family.   On the same terms, eh ?

GIOVANELLI.

Ah, no ; I don't want a rival !   (Reënter Mrs. Walker.)

MRS. WALKER, to Daisy.

I can't find the Consul; but as you're better it does n't matter.

DAISY.

I don't want the Consul: I want my mother.

MRS. WALKER.

I went to her room as well. Randolph had told her you were better, and so — and so — (Pausing, a little embarrassed, and looking round the circle.)

DAISY.

She is n't coming?

MRS. WALKER.

She has gone back to bed!

MRS. COSTELLO.

They *are* queer people, all the same!

MISS DURANT, to Mrs. Costello.

Shall we start for America now?

REVERDY.

Of course we shall — to be married!

WINTERBOURNE, laying his hand on Reverdy's shoulder.

We shall be married the same day. (To Daisy.) Shall we not, Daisy — in America?

DAISY, who has risen to her feet, leaning on his arm.

Oh, yes; you ought to go home!